Politics and History in Central Asia

Series Editor
Timur Dadabaev, University of Tsukuba, Tsukuba, Japan

In the past few decades, Central Asia has drawn the attention of academic and business communities as well as policy professionals because of its geostrategic importance (being located between Russia and China and in close proximity to Afghanistan, Pakistan, Iran, Turkey, and India), its international stability, and its rich energy resources. The region also faces challenges, such as post-conflict peacebuilding, impacts of the Afghan conflict, a number of recent inter-ethnic conflicts, and post-Socialist development paradigms. Approaching the problems and issues related to this region requires a multi-disciplinary perspective that takes into account political science, international relations, political economy, anthropology, geography, and security studies. The Politics and History in Central Asia series serves as a platform for emerging scholarship on this understudied region.

More information about this series at
https://link.springer.com/bookseries/14540

Nafissa Insebayeva

Modernity, Development and Decolonization of Knowledge in Central Asia

Kazakhstan as a Foreign Aid Provider

palgrave
macmillan

Nafissa Insebayeva
University of Tsukuba
Tsukuba, Japan

Politics and History in Central Asia
ISBN 978-981-16-5116-8 ISBN 978-981-16-5117-5 (eBook)
https://doi.org/10.1007/978-981-16-5117-5

This Palgrave Macmillan imprint is published by the registered company Springer Nature Singapore Pte Ltd.
The registered company address is: 152 Beach Road, #21-01/04 Gateway East, Singapore 189721, Singapore

Acknowledgements

First, I would like to dedicate this book to my late mother Nagima Insebayeva, who has always been the source of inspiration for me. Although her time on earth was short, she left an important legacy in our hearts and minds. She was a strong woman and a free spirit, who was not afraid to pursue her dreams, and I will forever admire her for that.

I want to thank my father Adilkhan Insebayev, without whom nothing I've ever achieved would've been possible. Although my mother's passing left my father alone, a young man with two little daughters to raise on his own, I can confidently say that he deserves the Best Parent Award. My father is my best friend, and he is the first feminist in my life. He raised me to be a leader, who is not afraid of defying expectations and going against social norms. He has always recognized the importance of education—not grades, but knowledge, and encouraged me to reach for the stars. The freedom I was given as a kid, the freedom without any conditions or limitations, allowed me to tap into different areas of interest without the fear of failure or rejection, and for that, I'm forever grateful.

Another person who has always served as my role model is my sister Sabina Insebayeva. I don't think there is anyone else who can ever come close to influencing and inspiring me as much as my sister does. We don't come from a privileged background, but thanks to my father and sister, I've never felt like something was out of reach for me. Sabina introduced me to everything I know and love: my first movies, my amazing English tutor, the life-changing Nazarbayev University. This book wouldn't be possible without her guidance either. Her contribution extends way beyond devoting hours to proofreading, sharing an immense amount of knowledge and providing insightful feedback, it's her moral support, care and encouragement during the most difficult times of my life that I appreciate the most.

I would also like to thank my mentor Professor Timur Dadabaev for the guidance I have received throughout the years. Professor Dadabaev's groundbreaking research and innovative approach always pushed me to challenge myself and think outside of the box. I believe Professor Dadabaev's Politics and History in Central Asia series with Palgrave is an amazing opportunity to look at our understudied region from a different perspective. I'm truly honored to have my first book be a part of this brilliant initiative.

Many thanks to Professor Toshinobu Usuyama and the Nippon Foundation Central Asia—Japan Human Resource Development Project (NipCA) for offering their kind support and creating a great environment, where young scholars can thrive and focus on producing high quality research. The project is a truly unique initiative of its kind, which aims to train the new generation of Central Asian leaders, and I am sure Professor Usuyama's vision will produce many prominent local experts, who will contribute to the development of the region in the future.

Of course, it is impossible not to extend my sincerest thanks to everyone who made it possible for me to undertake my field work in Kazakhstan. I would like to thank all national and international agencies and institutions who were willing to cooperate and assist me in conducting this research. This book would not be possible without your kind cooperation.

Finally, I must mention the international research community, both established scholars and young researchers, who were kind enough to offer me their thought-provoking insights and useful advice throughout the years. I am excited to witness the emergence of more experts, especially from the Central Asian region, who are redefining the status quo and introducing us to new, exciting findings.

Contents

Abbreviations

ADB	Asian Development Bank
CA	Central Asia
CEE	Central and Eastern Europe
CIS	Commonwealth of Independent States
DAC	Development Assistance Committee
DAG	Development Assistance Group
EU	European Union
GDP	Gross Domestic Product
GHA	Global Humanitarian Assistance
GIZ	German Society for International Cooperation
GNI	Gross National Income
GNP	Gross National Product
IBRD	International Bank for Reconstruction and Development
ICRC	International Committee of the Red Cross
IMF	International Monetary Fund
KazAID	Kazakh Agency for International Development
MFA	Ministry of Foreign Affairs of the Republic of Kazakhstan
MNE	Ministry of National Economy of the Republic of Kazakhstan
MoF	Ministry of Finance of the Republic of Kazakhstan
NSC	North-South Cooperation
OCHA	Office for the Coordination of Humanitarian Affairs
ODA	Official Development Assistance
OECD	Organization for Economic Cooperation and Development
ROCCA	Regional Office for the Caucasus and CA
SDG	Sustainable Development Goals
SSC	South-South Cooperation

UK	United Kingdom
UN	United Nations
UNDP	United Nations Development Programme
UNSC	United Nations Security Council
USA	United States of America
USSR	Union of Soviet Socialist Republic

List of Figures

CHAPTER 1

Introduction

Abstract This chapter introduces the reader to the debates surrounding Kazakhstan's emergence as the first official development assistance provider in the Central Asian region and starts the discussion on discourse theory, which serves as the foundation of the analysis in the subsequent chapters. The chapter presents a review of the contemporary foreign aid debate centered around the future of the international development landscape and specifically focuses on the encounter between "traditional"/"Northern" and "new"/"Southern" actors. The discussion draws attention to the existing discourses and practices in international development cooperation and lays the groundwork for the discussion of Kazakhstan's case as a foreign aid provider.

Keywords Kazakhstan · South-South development cooperation · Foreign policy · Emerging donors · Global North · Global South

The first decade after the collapse of the Soviet Union is often referred to as "the Dashing Nineties". For many, those were the years of frantic fight for basic survival. At the time many used every given opportunity to try to ensure a decent present and, perhaps, a decent future for us, the

N. Insebayeva, *Modernity, Development and Decolonization of Knowledge in Central Asia*, Politics and History in Central Asia,
https://doi.org/10.1007/978-981-16-5117-5_1

generation that had emerged among empty store shelves, galloping inflation and months of wage arrears. I vividly remember spending a chunk of my childhood selling Chinese jackets and blouses at the flea market. There was no feeling of shame or embarrassment associated with such entrepreneurial activities. It might have been due to my age or it might have been the other vendors standing next to us: my mother's friends and colleagues from the Karaganda Philharmonic Hall. During that period of time, a few cared or could afford to care about theaters, concert halls and cultural events.

I have a memory of my father coming home on a payday with a salary in the form of sugar, tea and macaroni. We did not ask any questions. My sister and I did our homework by candlelight and cooked with the neighbors in the communal yard. People used to build a fire in the middle of a football field (if that piece of land can be referred to as such) surrounded by apartment buildings. Everyone took turns cooking, since there was no light or gas in the houses. Everyone survived as best as they could.

There was a catastrophic shortage of money. Second-hand stores became particularly popular and were a dismal sight. There were piles of things in cramped quarters, often in semi-dark basements, and people had to dig through these piles to find a decent design or brand. In some of the "second-hand shops", things were sold by weight. For many, it was a worthy purchase, since buying 5 kg of clothing gave a good chance to find something worthy of attention in that shapeless assortment.

Shoppers would come to such stores early in the morning for a chance to find or get interesting things. The specific smell and the general atmosphere of those lowbrow flea markets have permanently cemented in the minds of post-Soviet citizens a perception of second-hand goods as shameful and undesirable.

At a certain point, it has become a habit for people to not mention where their new pieces of clothes arrived from. Salespeople used to say that the items came from America and Europe. This was how the "West" was helping developing countries. The assistance they have provided came in different forms, including clothing. It was an anxious, difficult and poor time, but for our Soviet parents everything was compensated by freedom and hope.

More than 30 years have passed since then, and new times seem to have come. The current generation is the generation of the era of change, the generation that was born in a new state, with new territories, a new constitution and a new president.

The Arrival of a New Donor

In December 2014, Kazakhstan became the first official development assistance (ODA) provider in the Central Asian region. By doing so, Kazakhstan has officially changed from being a recipient of official aid to a donor country. Despite the fact that this event is historic for Kazakhstan's development, the phenomenon remains largely understudied.

Much research has revolved around foreign policy motivations for the provision of Kazakhstan's development assistance. For instance, most studies in the field suggest that Kazakh foreign aid practices are largely driven by economic, political and strategic objectives. In line with this, the key motivating factors for Kazakh foreign assistance provision are typically framed along the following spectrum: from regional security and economic concerns[1] and aspirations for regional leadership[2] to "external legitimization" intentions[3] and the desire to maximize its soft power.[4] This emphasis on motives for Kazakh aid in the relevant literature is explained by the widespread conceptualization of foreign aid as an instrument for achieving donors' foreign policy interests.[5]

As a result, most of these studies are rooted in rationalist understanding and are largely concerned with examining how Kazakhstan as a self- interested rational actor pursues its interests strategically, rather than inquiring where those interests and preferences come from.[6]

Thus, despite some useful research on the motivations behind Kazakhstan's aid giving, very little is known about **how Kazakhstan has emerged as a development cooperation provider**, and most importantly **what *kind* of new actor in development Kazakhstan has become. What kind of ideas, norms, values, discourses and practices has this actor adopted and why?**

The purpose of this book is to address these research questions that have been left entirely out of account in the existing literature. It should be noted, however, that answers to such questions do not just make a novel ***empirical contribution*** to scholarship on Kazakhstan and Central Asia.

Initially, this research attempted to fill the aforementioned vacuum of critical knowledge on "new"/"emerging" donors, focusing on Kazakhstan, as a non-first tier aid provider. Later on, however, questions about Kazakhstan's transition from a recipient to a development aid provider gradually led this inquiry to wider issues of Soviet/Western modernity and coloniality and its relevance for development practices in the post-Soviet space, which will be discussed in more details in the following chapters.

By focusing on Kazakhstan as a previously understudied case to explain provision of foreign aid, the book also makes a major ***conceptual contribution*** to international scholarship on the increasingly polycentric structure of the international development landscape in which "new actors" have begun to play an increasingly active and important role.

In the literature, "new actors" in international development are often referred to as "emerging donors", "non-DAC donors" and "Southern donors". These labels have often been used as a shorthand to set those new actors apart from the Organization for Economic Cooperation and Development's (OECD) Development Assistance Committee (DAC) members who are often referred to as "established donors", "traditional donors", or "Western/Northern donors".[7]

Despite its relatively wide usage, however, many commentators have pointed out that the categorization of such actors as "new" or "emerging" is quite imprecise.[8]

Firstly, many of these "new/emerging" actors are not novices in the field of development assistance (e.g., China, India, Brazil).[9] For example, China's aid-like activities commenced soon after its establishment in 1949 with the first initiatives in Africa dating back to the 1950s.[10]

Secondly, the existing umbrella terms may misleadingly entail a connotation of homogeneity among "new" development aid providers and disregard substantial differences among them.[11] Furthermore, while new development actors are diverse, by the same token, traditional actors are not homogeneous.[12] Often they diverge in the way they organize their aid and prioritize aid's purposes.[13] For instance, French international aid policies and development programs have been argued to target former French colonies and French-speaking countries for the purpose of maintaining a sphere of influence in those regions, while Denmark has been reported to have used its aid to further the country's commercial goals and secure access to raw materials in recipient states.[14] Another good example comes from Japan, which despite being regarded as an "established" donor is still often criticized for not meeting certain expectations of the DAC community coordinated aid.[15] For instance, over the years, Japan's ODA scheme has been met with significant criticisms for the tied nature of its development efforts abroad.[16]

Indeed, "new" providers constitute as diverse and heterogeneous a group of actors as do the "old" donors. However, they appear to be held together through the process of collective identity building. Viewed in this light, "old"/"traditional"/"Northern" and "new"/"emerging"/"Southern" development actors can be conceived as members of "imagined communities",[17] whose boundaries are shaped and reshaped through the process of "Othering".

As such, providers of development cooperation, regardless of their diversity, draw lines of differences not only according to material characteristics, but through the prism of ideas, norms, values and identities.[18]

The dominant narrative framings of the OECD-DAC aid and South-South development cooperation (SSC) exemplify the point. Traditional Northern donors adopt the OECD-DAC assistance approach and have historically been operating under a North-South logic, according to which aid from "a rich and powerful North" has to be transferred to "the poor and marginalized South".[19]

More precisely, the narratives embraced by the countries of "the Global North" emphasize charity and moral obligation toward "the less fortunate Global South",[20] transfer of expertise based on the Northern "superior" knowledge and the virtues of suspending recipients' obligation to reciprocate. In this context, the "North/South" divide is used not to denote a geographical space, but rather has been employed metaphorically to highlight "a chain of interconnected socioeconomic and political claims that sustained a global landscape of normalized hierarchies".[21]

The SSC framework, on the contrary, takes its roots in the Bandung Conference of 1955 and promotes a vision of emancipatory, state-led development with the Global South working in solidarity against the Global North.[22] Hence, the SSC narratives, embraced by Southern donors, have typically stressed principles of solidarity and equality between partners, sharing knowledge based on experience, political non-interference and the virtue of mutual benefit and recognition of reciprocity.[23] SSC, defined as "the transfer or exchange of financial resources, technology, personnel and/or knowledge" between the countries of the "global South", in fact, helps to "foster a common Southern identity, one based on solidarity, and its distinctiveness from exploitative North-South relations".[24] Therefore, as Ndlovu-Gatsheni and Tafira (2018)[25] noted "what exists today as the 'global South' and the 'global North' were simultaneous inventions through the operationalization of the paradigm of difference".

In this regard, even though SSC providers are highly heterogeneous in terms of priorities, policies, institutional arrangements, and engagement with international forums and initiatives,[26] "they often draw on claims of shared colonial and postcolonial experiences, and frequently anchor their activities within a wider framework of promoting the collective strength of the South vis-à-vis the North".[27] It could, therefore, be said that the common denominator these "new" actors share is their desire "to preserve their 'Southern' identity",[28] which differs from that of the Northern "Others". As Fiddian-Qasmiyeh and Daley (2018)[29] have further put it, "the contrast with the established aid system [North–South aid paradigm], rooted in the colonial legacy and reproducing unequal international relations" is at the core of Southern identity.[30]

The encounter between these "old"/"Northern" and "new"/"Southern" actors, discourses and practices in development cooperation has triggered an impressive wave of interesting research,[31] generating heated debate over the future of the international development regime.

The emergence of "new" or so-called non-DAC donors has changed the international foreign aid landscape.[32] For instance, some scholars argue that an increasing heterogeneity of the global aid regime with the emergence of new providers is evident.[33] Others describe traditional donors as declining powers and/or suggest that the effectiveness of the efforts led by the OECD has been declining with non-DAC donors gaining increasing prominence on the global foreign aid arena.[34]

Thus, the "emerging donors" have been attracting increasing worldwide attention as they quickly broaden their global presence and activities, and make considerable changes both in individual recipient states and in the international aid community, which has long been dominated by the nexus of DAC of the OECD and the World Bank.[35] Some scholars postulate that "new" donors may potentially provide additional sources of funding and diversify the portfolio of solutions and strategies to development and poverty eradication.[36] Others, on the contrary, expressed concern with the distinctive aid philosophies and forms of aid-giving practices adopted by these non-traditional donors, emphasizing the potential negative effect non-traditional donors' aid strategies might have on its recipients (e.g., erosion of debt sustainability, quality of governance, environmental safety).

What a great number of available studies come short of is that they tend to analyze the foreign aid landscape with applying a dichotomous approach (traditional vs. emerging donors) to the issue, which arguably limits that scope of research needed to understand the changing dynamics in international aid architecture.

In other words, as it has been previously mentioned, it is important to keep in mind that similarly to traditional donors, emerging donors are not a monolithic group and are rather diverse in their approaches to international development assistance.[37] Thus, it is not only the DAC members that the emerging donors have intrinsic differences with, but other emerging donors as well. What they have in common though is not only their commitment to pursue a non-traditional path of aid-giving, but also their identity as previous (or current) recipients of international assistance. Many see this as an advantage due to the belief that these donors can successfully utilize their "recipient-knowledge" and experience when dealing with their counterparts, which can result in positive development outcomes.[38]

Diverging views on development policies have led to existing fractures and contradictions among and within the members of the OECD-DAC and SSC donors. While the OECD-DAC was once perceived to have held a preeminent status in defining purposes of development and how to achieve it, the Southern providers have been increasingly undermining the dominant position of Northern aid by offering new modes of behavior and distinguished views on development that challenge the current state of affairs in international development architecture.[39]

Given these considerations, the questions of who the new actors are, what ideas they bring to development and how they respond to existing ones gain more significance.

Hence, taking into account that development landscape is becoming increasingly polycentric,[40] it is somewhat surprising that research in the field of development cooperation has yet to examine the full diversity of new actors. While some emerging donors became the subject of intense scrutiny and discussion (e.g., BRICS), others are often left aside. As a result, there is still a vacuum of critical knowledge informed by fieldwork regarding not-less-important cohorts of the second-tier providers.[41] This is particularly puzzling, given that these often-overlooked actors also contribute to the changing global balance of power through strengthening their positions as regional and area-specific powerhouses (e.g., MIKTA[42]). While middle-income countries by definition face significant barriers, such as demographic, political and economic weight, to competitively engage in every aspect of global affairs, they nevertheless are capable of playing important and active roles within certain policies, arenas and geographies. The relatively smaller size of these actors does not necessarily jeopardize their strategic importance and their ability to have a significant impact on regional and global trends and developments. In fact, apart from being a potential source of funding and resources, such key regional players often offer context-sensitive local expertise, as well as serve as important providers of linguistic and cultural understanding and historical ties, which sets them further apart from the traditional donor camp.

Their qualitative divergence from the aforementioned BRICS presents fundamental challenges at theory and conceptualization level, which calls for a more detailed analysis and a greater understanding of such multidimensional phenomena as second-tier providers, which remain highly undertheorized and under analyzed.

In confronting this situation, this book examines the emergence of Kazakhstan as a foreign aid provider. Transcending the usually accepted typology of donor countries, I argue that Kazakhstan represents an interesting new type of foreign aid provider—neither "Northern" nor "Southern. By highlighting the limitations of this common framing of the development industry, this study makes a valuable contribution to the literature on international development.

Methodological Overview

Methodologically speaking, the work draws on qualitative and quantitative data. It must be noted that data available for Kazakhstan's ODA activities remains limited in important ways, as there is a lack of established, transparent and coordinated mechanisms in disclosing and reporting information regarding the country's aid-giving. This implies that conducting quantitative analysis typical in the existing aid literature is not a feasible option for this research. As such, this research adopts a discourse analysis as a method of analyzing Kazakh aid through examining primary sources such as official statements, speeches and archival documents, conducting interviews in Kazakh, Russian and English, in addition to surveying secondary sources, such as articles on foreign aid as well as available statistics.

Interviews were chosen as one of the major sources of qualitative data for this research, as they served as a vital piece of data that shed light on the events prior to and discourses behind the official rhetoric on foreign aid, which, in turn, allowed for tracking the determinants of the resulting policy decisions. As such, by utilizing this method, the author was able to uncover insights not disclosed in the official public statements. On top of that, the case of Kazakh ODA remains understudied mainly due to the limited information regarding the subject that has been made available to the general public. Hence, most information regarding Kazakhstan's aid modality and development utilized in this study is primary data obtained by the author through the interview process.

Structured, semi-structured and open-ended interviews were conducted with (a) current government officials and diplomats directly involved in strategizing and implementing Kazakh aid policy and (b) experts from international non-governmental organizations that assist Kazakhstan with the realization and evaluation of its development initiatives. More specifically,interviews were conducted with Kazakh high-ranking government officials (at the level of the former Minister of Foreign Affairs (MFA RK)), employees of international organizations and agencies (UNDP), MASHAV (former Israeli Ambassador to Kazakhstan (2015–2018), JICA (program managers)).

The open-ended question format often resulted in several previously unconsidered topics entering the research agenda. Interviews were structured around the main themes of the study, including but not exclusively centering on the historical origins of Kazakhstan's foreign aid policy, as well as Kazakhstan's cooperation with other foreign aid donors. Most interviews were conducted in an official setting, while a few were collected during informal conversations. The author made sure to obtain consent of all participating parties, whose remarks and recollections are used in the book.

The fieldwork was spread out over the research period from 2017 to 2019 when the author paid multiple visits to Kazakhstan to collect most recent information on Kazakhstan's ODA activities, conduct archival work and deepen the current understanding about Kazakhstan's foreign aid policy.

The archival research was for the most part conducted at the "Archive of the First President of the Republic of Kazakhstan" and "Kazakhstan's Central State Archive". The choice of these particular repositories is based on the fact that the materials of the Soviet period comprise the bulk of their archival depository.

The information presented in the documents of the Soviet period reflects the main stages in the formation of Kazakh republic's industrial base, the creation of its economy, the development of virgin and fallow lands, the course and characteristics of culture-building, demographic and ethnic changes, and many other issues.

Other primary data sources include official statements, speeches, think tank reports and press releases related to Kazakhstan's foreign aid. Discourse analysis has been applied to official documents such as the "Law on Official Development Assistance", "The Concept of the Republic of Kazakhstan in the sphere of official development assistance", "Plan of the Nation", "Foreign Policy Concept 2014–2020", "State policy in the field of ODA for 2017–2020" and other relevant primary sources on Kazakhstan's foreign policy and foreign aid, including but not limited to the Annual Addresses of the President of Kazakhstan. Statistical data for the most part was sourced from the OECD database, as well as the Kazakh Ministry of Foreign Affairs and Ministry of Finance. As for the secondary data, the author primarily relied on the respected scholarly works on theories of international relations, the trends in foreign aid and Kazakhstan's foreign policy.

Book Outline

This chapter introduced the reader to the debates surrounding Kazakhstan's foreign aid and started a discussion on discourse theory—the theory used to conduct the analysis in the subsequent chapters. The chapter reviewed the contemporary foreign aid debate centered around the future of the international development regime, specifically focusing on the encounter between "traditional"/"Northern" and "new"/"Southern" actors, discourses and practices in development cooperation in order to lay the groundwork for the discussion of Kazakhstan's case.

Chapter 2 looks at the concept of development, whose roots lie in deep historical processes of modernity/coloniality and capitalism that gained prominence in the wake of the world's decolonization and reordering in the aftermath of World War II. By deconstructing the concept of "development", this chapter demonstrates that the Global North/Global South, developed/developing, the First World/the Third World countries lie at the core of theorization about North-South (N-S) and South-South (S-S) aid paradigms and set the scene for the analysis of Kazakhstan's case in Chapter 6. Building on this discussion, this chapter explores the reasons why the existing literature on foreign aid is mainly concerned with "old"/Northern and "new"/Southern donors. It proceeds to contend that Kazakhstan does not fit either of these categories and in fact stands as an "outlier" falling outside any of these groups due to its historical experiences. In this regard, the chapter advances several arguments for why this study finds the practice of incorporating Kazakhstan into the new/Southern providers group rather problematic.

Chapter 3 provides a discussion and a brief overview of the history of aid, as well as the main narratives that dominate the literature on development and humanitarian aid provision. This part of the book serves to shed light on existing studies on Kazakh aid.

Chapter 4 explores the activities of Kazakhstan as an aid provider. Having a long-standing record of offering emergency relief and humanitarian aid to foreign countries, Kazakhstan entered the emerging donors' camp in 2013 and was quick to dramatically increase its ODA budget over the years to come. The chapter discusses the constructed aid modality and highlights the main features and characteristics of Kazakhstan's ODA system. It starts with providing an overview of Kazakhstan's activities as a humanitarian aid donor and moves to the section on the adoption of relevant legislation pertaining to official development assistance.

Chapter 5 focuses on Kazakhstan's pre-independence history and takes a closer look at the peculiarities of the Soviet modernization project. Chapter 6 is based on the primary sources uncovered by the author in the archives in Kazakhstan and highlights the development programs implemented on the territory of modern-day Kazakhstan by the Soviet regime. This chapter examines whether particular aspects of Kazakhstan's history have affected its subsequent foreign aid policy choices, and if so, then how. Specifically, the Soviet emphasis on education and female emancipation will be discussed as the primary sources of influence for Kazakhstan's current development efforts abroad. The work shows that the Soviet legacy represents a crucial element, which has affected Kazakhstan's conceptualization and understanding of development. In other words, this chapter will analyze Kazakhstan's development aid projects in Central Asia and Afghanistan and will provide an explanation for how these programs have been influenced by Kazakhstan's identity as a former Soviet republic, aid recipient and ODA provider.

In Chapter 6, the author will turn to discussing Kazakhstan's experience as a foreign aid recipient in the years following its independence and its transition into an ODA donor. Over the years, Kazakhstan has transitioned from a recipient of Moscow's donations under the Soviet rule to a benefactor of Western development aid in the 1990s. Given Kazakhstan's unique experiences as a constituent and independent republic, a foreign aid recipient and an aid provider, this chapter will argue that international donors have played a significant role in shaping Kazakhstan's development path and have impacted its policy choices regarding its foreign aid activities. More specifically, the study argues that the Western aid has majorly influenced Kazakhstan's own development strategy during the 2000s and, subsequently, its foreign aid policy in early 2010s. In particular, the discussion in the first part of this chapter emphasizes the link between knowledge acquired by the Kazakh leadership at different stages of the state's development and policies that the Kazakh government has eventually produced. The discussion provides a brief explanation of Kazakhstan's decision to cut its dependence on foreign aid in the early 2000s and to adhere to the self-reliance principle, which the Western donorship has been an important determinant of. This section will explain how international factors have influenced Kazakhstan's current ODA system. Finally, Chapter 7 will conclude the discussion by summarizing the key findings of the study in relation to the research aims presented in the earlier chapters.

Notes

1. Mirzayan, G. (2014). Kazakhstan formiruet poyas dobrososedstva [Kazakhstan is forming the belt of a good neighbourhood]. *Expert Online*. http://expert.ru/2014/11/13/kazahstan-formiruet-poyas-dobrososedstva/.
2. De Cordier, B. (2014). Kazakhstan and Azerbaijan as donors of humanitarian aid: Has the diversification of aid channels and donors reached Southern Eurasia? *Central Asia and the Caucasus, 15*(4).
3. Posega, P. (2015). Kazakhstan beyond Borat. *Modern Diplomacy*. http://moderndiplomacy.eu/index.php?option=com_k2&view=item&id=763:kazakhstan-beyond-borat&Itemid=772.
4. Malyshev, D., & Bainazarova, E. (2016). Russia and Kazakhstan: Mutually different interests for regional leadership. In H. Rytövuori-Apunen, *The regional security puzzle around Afghanistan: Bordering practices in Central Asia and beyond* (1st ed., pp. 243–270). Barbara Budrich Publishers.

5. McKinlay, R. D., & Mughan, A. (1984). *Aid and arms to the third world: An analysis of the distribution and import of US official transfer*. St. Martin's; Morgenthau, H. (1962). A political theory of foreign aid. *American Political ScienceReview, 56*(2), 301–309; Hook, S. W. (1995). *National Interest and Foreign Aid*. Lynne Rienner Publishers.
6. Wendt, A. (1999). *Social theory of international politics*. Cambridge University Press.
7. Seifert, J. (2016). New dynamics or old patterns? South-South Cooperation between Brazil and Angola. In J. van der Merwe, I. Taylor, & A. Arkhangelskaya, *Emerging powers in Africa: A new wave in the relationship?* (1st ed., pp. 129–157). Palgrave Macmillan; Kim, S., & Lightfoot, S. (2011). Does "DAC-ability" really matter? The emergence of non-DAC donors: Introduction to policy arena. *Journal of International Development, 23*, 711–721. https://doi.org/10.1002/jid.1795; Woods, N. (2008). Whose aid? Whose influence? China, emerging donors and the silent revolution in development assistance. *International Affairs, 84*(6), 1205–1221.
8. Chin, G., & Quadir, F. (2012). Introduction: Rising states, rising donors and the global aid regime. *Cambridge Review of International Affairs, 25*(4), 493–506.
9. Kragelund, P. (2019). *South-South Development* (1st ed.). Routledge; Chin, G., & Quadir, F. (2012). Introduction: Rising states, rising donors and the global aid regime. *Cambridge Review of International Affairs, 25*(4), 493–506.
10. Woods, N. (2008). Whose aid? Whose influence? China, emerging donors and the silent revolution in development assistance. *International Affairs, 84*(6), 1205–1221.
11. Fejerskov, A., Lundsgaarde, E., & Cold-Ravnkilde, S. (2016). Uncovering the dynamics of interaction in development cooperation: A review of the "new actors in development" research agenda. *DIIS Working Papers, 1*, 1–24; Kragelund, P. (2015). Towards convergence and cooperation in the global development finance regime: Closing Africa's policy space. *Cambridge Review Of International Affairs, 28*(2), 246–262; Rowlands, D. (2012). Individual BRICS or a collective bloc? Convergence and divergence amongst 'emerging donor' nations. *Cambridge Review of International Affairs, 25*(4), 629–649.

12. Yamada, S. (2016). *Post-education-for-all and sustainable development paradigm* (1st ed.). Emerald Group Publishing Limited.
13. Lancaster, C. (2007). *Foreign aid: Diplomacy, development, domestic politics*. University of Chicago Press.
14. Lancaster, C. (2009). Sixty years of foreign aid: What have we learned? *International Journal, 64*(3), New Perspectives on Canadian Security Studies (Summer, 2009), pp. 799–810.
15. Wissenbach, U. (2010). A new Seoul consensus on development: The G20 needs to reconcile effective ODA with emerging country economic cooperation. In T. Fues & P. Wolff, *G20 and Global Development: How can the new summit architecture promote pro-poor growth and sustainability?* (1st ed., pp. 26–29). German Development Institute.
16. Arase, D. (Ed.). (2005). *Japan's foreign aid: Old continuities and new directions*. Routledge.
17. Anderson, B. (1983). *Imagined Communities* (1st ed). Verso.
18. Lancaster, C. (2007). *Foreign aid: Diplomacy, development, domestic politics*. University of Chicago Press.
19. Williams, G., Meth, P., & Willis, K. (2009). *Geographies of developing areas: The Global South in a changing world* (1st ed.). Routledge.
20. The phrase 'Global South' refers broadly to the regions of Latin America, Asia, Africa and Oceania. It is one of a family of terms, including "Third World" and "Periphery" that denote regions outside Europe and North America, mostly (though not all) low-income and often politically or culturally marginalized.
21. Lauria, V., & Fumagalli, C. (2019). BRICS, the southern model and the evolving landscape of development assistance: Toward a new taxonomy. *Public Administration and Development, 39*(4–5), 215–230.
22. Engel, S. (2019). South-South Cooperation in Southeast Asia: From Bandung and Solidarity to Norms and Rivalry. *Journal of Current Southeast Asian Affairs, 38*(2), 218–242.
23. Gulrajani, N., & Swiss, L. (2018). Donor proliferation to what ends? New donor countries and the search for legitimacy. *Canadian Journal of Development Studies/Revue canadienne d'études du développement*; Mawdsley, E. (2012). *From recipients*.

24. Aneja, U. (2018). South-South cooperation and competition. In E. Fiddian-Qasmiyeh & P. Daley, *Routledge handbook of South-South relations* (1st ed., pp. 141–152). Routledge.
25. Ndlovu-Gatsheni, S., & Tafira, K. (2018). The invention of the Global South and the politics of South-South solidarity. In E. Fiddian-Qasmiyeh & P. Daley, *Routledge handbook of South-South relations* (1st ed.). Routledge.
26. Renzio, P., & Seifert, J. (2014). South-South cooperation and the future of development assistance: Mapping actors and options. *Third World Quarterly, 35*(10), 1860–1875.
27. Mawdsley, E., Fourie, E., & Nauta, W. (2019). *Researching South-South development cooperation* (1st ed). Routledge.
28. Chin, G., & Quadir, F. (2012). Introduction: Rising states, rising donors and the global aid regime. *Cambridge Review of International Affairs, 25*(4), 493–506 (p. 500).
29. Fiddian-Qasmiyeh, E., & Daley, P. (2018). *Routledge handbook of South-South relations* (1st ed.). Routledge.
30. The above discussion of the dominant narrative framings of OECD-DAC aid and SSC does not represent an argument in favor of grouping "new" and "old" actors into binary classification. Rather, the idea here is to demonstrate that the identity problematique (that goes along with other factors, such as values and norms) should be put at the core of the research agenda in the field of development cooperation. After all, identities (that are conditioned by non-material structures) inform actors' interests, which, in turn, guide their behavior in terms of development provision (see Reus-Smit, 2013).
31. Fejerskov, A., Lundsgaarde, E., & Cold-Ravnkilde, S. (2016). Uncovering the dynamics of interaction in development cooperation: A review of the "new actors in development" research agenda. *DIIS Working Papers, 1*, 1–24; Mawdsley, E. (2018). Southern leaders, Northern followers? Who has 'socialized' whom in international development? In E. Fiddian-Qasmiyeh & P. Daley, *Routledge handbook of South-South relations* (1st ed.). Routledge.
32. Manning, R. (2006). Will "emerging donors" change the face of international cooperation? *Development Policy Review, 24*(4), 371–385. http://www.oecd.org/dac/36417541.pdf.

33. Woods, N. (2008). Whose aid? Whose influence? China, emerging donors and the silent revolution in development assistance. *International Affairs, 84*(6), 1205–1221.
34. Lancaster, C. (2007). *Foreign aid: Diplomacy, development, domestic politics*. University of Chicago Press.
35. Shimomura, Y., & Ping, W. (2015). *Chains of knowledge creation and emerging donors* (JICA-RI Working Papers 88). https://www.jica.go.jp/jica-ri/publication/workingpaper/jrft3q000000262n-att/JICA-RI_WP_No.88.pdf.
36. Shimomura, Y., & Ping, W. (2015). *Chains of knowledge creation and emerging donors* (JICA-RI Working Papers 88). https://www.jica.go.jp/jica-ri/publication/workingpaper/jrft3q000000262n-att/JICA-RI_WP_No.88.pdf.
37. Walz, J., & Ramachandran, V. (2011). *Brave new world: A literature review of emerging donors and the changing nature of foreign assistance* (Center for Global Development Working Paper 273). https://www.cgdev.org/publication/brave-new-world-literature-review-emerging-donors-and-changing-nature-foreign-assistance.
38. Shimomura, Y., & Ping, W. (2015). *Chains of knowledge creation and emerging donors* (JICA-RI Working Papers 88). https://www.jica.go.jp/jica-ri/publication/workingpaper/jrft3q000000262n-att/JICA-RI_WP_No.88.pdf.
39. Eyben, R., & Savage, L. (2012). Emerging and submerging powers: Imagined geographies in the new development partnership at the Busan Fourth High Level Forum. *Journal of Development Studies, 49*(4), 457–469.
40. Kragelund, P. (2015). Towards convergence and cooperation in the global development finance regime: Closing Africa's policy space. *Cambridge Review of International Affairs, 28*(2), 246–262; Fejerskov, A., Lundsgaarde, E., & Cold-Ravnkilde, S. (2016). Uncovering the dynamics of interaction in development cooperation: A review of the "new actors in development" research agenda. *DIIS Working Papers, 1*, 1–24; Mawdsley, E. (2018). Southern leaders, Northern followers? Who has 'socialized' whom in international development? In E. Fiddian-Qasmiyeh & P. Daley, *Routledge handbook of South-South relations* (1st ed.). Routledge.
41. For discussion, see Bergamaschi, I., Moore, P., & Tickner, A. (2017). *South-South cooperation beyond the myths: Rising*

donors, new aid practices? (1st ed.). Palgrave Macmillan; Mawdsley, E. (2012). *From recipients to donors: Emerging powers and the changing development landscape* (1st ed.). Zed Books; Scott, J., vom Hau, M., & Hulme, D. (2010). *Beyond the BRICS: Identifying the "emerging middle powers" and understanding their role in global poverty reduction* (Working Paper, BWPI, 137); Jaffrelot, Ch. (2009). *Emerging states: The wellspring of a new world order*. Columbia University Press; Sato, J., Shiga, H., Kobayashi, T., & Kondoh, H. (2010). *How do "emerging" donors differ from "traditional" donors? An institutional analysis of foreign aid*. Retrieved from JICA-RI Website https://www.jica.go.jp/jica-ri/publication/workingpaper/jrft3q00000022dd-att/JICA-RI_WP_No.2_2010.pdf.

42. MIKTA is an informal consultation and coordination platform among Mexico, Indonesia, South Korea, Turkey and Australia. For more information, please visit http://www.mikta.org/about/history.php.

CHAPTER 2

Setting the Stage for Research: Theoretical Approaches to Development

Abstract This chapter explores the concept of development, whose roots lie in deep historical processes of modernity/coloniality and capitalism, which gained prominence in the wake of the world's decolonization and reordering in the aftermath of the World War II. By deconstructing the concept of "development", this chapter demonstrates that the Global North/Global South, developed/developing, the First World/the Third World countries lie at the core of theorization about North-South (N-S) and South-South (S-S) aid paradigms and sets the scene for the analysis of Kazakhstan's case. Building on this discussion, this chapter explores the reasons why the existing literature on foreign aid in mainly concerned with "old"/Northern and "new"/Southern donors. It proceeds to contend that Kazakhstan does not fit either of the categories and in fact stands as an "outlier" falling outside any of these groups due to its historical experiences. In this regard, the chapter advances several arguments for why this study finds the practice of incorporating Kazakhstan into the new/Southern providers group rather problematic.

Keywords Coloniality · Development · Modernity · Underdeveloped · Third World · Soviet Union

N. Insebayeva, *Modernity, Development and Decolonization of Knowledge in Central Asia*, Politics and History in Central Asia,
https://doi.org/10.1007/978-981-16-5117-5_2

The concept of development, whose roots lie in deep historical processes of modernity/coloniality and capitalism, gained prominence in the wake of the world's decolonization and reordering in the aftermath of World War II. At the time, albeit unenthusiastically, the European colonizing powers (e.g., the British Empire, France) had started to accept the changing realities in the global structures and began to reluctantly inch in the direction of decolonization. Eventually, independence movements and decolonization efforts in former colonies, as well as the lack of financial resources and sufficient political support in Europe to sustain its colonial rule, resulted in the gradual dissolution of overseas empires across Asia, Africa and the Caribbean.[1] This is how a "world of nations" replaced (at least nominally) the colonial world.[2]

The widespread euphoria and a wave of excitement that greeted the newly obtained "freedom" in former dependent territories were partially clouded by the urgent necessity to create jobs, revenue, establish necessary institutions and provide social services to the population among other concerns. This time of uncertainty seemed to call for "development" as the answer to the pressing demands new governments have faced.

One of the characteristics of that period was the widespread belief that the newly independent states could catch up with the "developed world" only if they mimicked "modern" Western countries. The rapid recovery of post-war Europe further fueled that kind of thinking. It was believed that all societies were moving along a linear path toward "modernity" and "development".

Given that Western countries claimed themselves furthest advanced along this path, it was suggested that the adoption of social, economic and political systems developed in the West would eventually allow "developing" nations to progress into "developed" industrial states.[3] This line of thought emphasized the Western experience of industrialization, which was synonymous with *world* industrialization at the time, as an engine of economic growth, which would help poor countries change the unfortunate conditions of their economies. It was widely assumed that as their economies grew, wealth would trickle down to the masses.

Development, as Sachs (1992, p. 1)[4] eloquently summarized, was understood as "the idea which oriented emerging nations in their journey through post-war history. No matter whether democracies or dictatorships, the countries of the South proclaimed development as their primary aspiration, after they had been freed from colonial subordination".

After the disintegration of the colonial empires, the USA took the initiative to lead the world and "lighten the burden" of the "least fortunate"[5] by enunciating a new direction for American foreign policy and launching, what came to be universally known as the "Point Four program".

> "We must embark on a bold new program for making the benefits of our scientific advances and industrial progress available for the improvement and growth of **underdeveloped areas**. More than half of the people of the world are living in conditions approaching misery. Their food is inadequate. They are victims of disease. Their economic life is primitive and stagnant. Their poverty is a handicap and a threat both to them and to more prosperous areas". (Truman, 1949)

Believed to be "at the top of the social evolutionary scale",[6] the USA announced its commitment in redressing "the economic backwardness and political instability that plagued underdeveloped regions of the world".[7] This is when the notion of underdevelopment appeared for the first time, dividing the world into "the haves" and the "have-nots", and this is how the idea of "Third World Aid" was launched.[8]

In this sense, the Point Four Program can be conceptualized as the point of departure of developmentalism "as a field of discourse".[9] Accordingly, the industrialized countries of the Global North were considered to be ***developed***, while the other countries, specifically those of Asia, Africa and Latin America, came to be "invented" as the ***underdeveloped*** Third World.[10]

This implied that the latter required specific assistance and interventions from the former to embark upon the path toward industrialization and modernization, which often manifested through the transfer of Northern "superior" capital, technology and knowledge to the South. Such interventions in the forms of development projects and programs were designed in accordance with expert knowledge pertaining to development tools and strategies, as well as improvement of quality of life based on the Western experience. This drive for development and the increasing interest in providing aid "to those in need", however, are not explained by altruistic motives.

At the time many theorized that the growing influence of the communist superpower—the Soviet Union, which managed to industrialize outside of capitalism—pushed the "First World" (USA) to search for supporters among newly independent states, which were quickly labeled as Third World nations, in order to sustain its struggle for global supremacy. Just like that "modernization theory started to compete with communism in a world split by the Cold War"[11] and the concept of development has become a weapon in the decades-long competition between two distinct political systems based on opposing ideologies.[12]

However, by the 1980s to mid-1990s, the scholarly community began to question the validity of the developmental discourse[13] In fact, the very meaning of development, which was previously seen as "verifiable and desirable",[14] became the object of much criticism and suspicion.

Some scholars, for instance, called for the dismissal of the concept and practice of the so-called development,[15] denouncing it "as a threat [...] masked by illusions",[16] which leads to "a tremendous loss of diversity"[17] and "disastrous consequences for those supposed to benefit" from it.[18] Rahnema (1997) explicitly mentioned that a new form of colonization was hidden under the convenient label of development and progress. It has been argued that decolonization did not just end with the transfer of political power from the colonizer to the colonized,[19] because colonial authority never rested on juridical control alone.[20] "The mental space", as Sachs (1992, p. 4) argued, "in which people dream and act [was largely] occupied by Western imagery". All along, development was nothing else than the Westernization of the world.[21]

In line with this thinking, development was interpreted by many as intimately linked to modernization, which as a result led to the extension of the Western domination and its nationalist allies in the developing countries.[22] Under such circumstances, development became the main focus of discussions on the so-called Third World countries, "achieving the status of a certainty in the social imaginary".[23] Development as a discourse of Western origin has grown from "colonial discourse, which was its direct predecessor regarding the conceptualization of the South from a Northern perspective".[24] In a sense, development operated "as a powerful mechanism for the cultural, social and economic production of the Third World" (ibid.).

In the 1990s, scholars were highly preoccupied with the question of whether decolonizing knowledge and its production, i.e., separating it from its grounding in colonialism, was possible at all.[25] In pursuit of answers to these questions, the long-lasting impact of colonialism on development has started to get acknowledged. A wave of postcolonial studies concerned with historical processes started to shed light on currently observed trends and policies in development cooperation. While there remained a great necessity to find effective approaches to tackling poverty, inequality and other challenges across the globe, postcolonial theory called for further examination of chosen efforts to ascertain whether those were a continuation of postcolonial relationships.

Postcolonial theories thus have been developed to capture, analyze and highlight the complex relationship and links between current discourses and colonial patterns. As such, one of the primary objectives of postcolonial studies is not to simply salvage the past, but to show that coloniality remains an active force in the present and continues to shape the world. In other words, postcolonialism is preoccupied with explaining that to this day many, if not all, aspects of modern societies still harbor colonial influences; moreover, it points at the persistence of a power relationship between the developed nations of the West and their former colonies.[26] According to postcolonial studies, hierarchical social structures in world affairs are created and maintained by binary oppositions, such as the "we-they" and "North-South" dichotomies, in which the opposites derive their significance from their oppositional relationship to each other.

Following on from the discussion above, it can be concluded that despite some notable areas of divergence, both development and postcolonial studies are concerned about the "global South" and North/South relations. Classical approaches to development (e.g., modernization, dependency theories), despite representing "different points in the spectrum of approaches to international development",[27] share in common "the unconditional belief in the concept of progress" and "the idea of a homogeneous Third World".[28] Modernization from poverty, backwardness and underdevelopment toward Western modernity was believed to be a linear process, which happens in the same way for all countries.

In postcolonial writings, on the other hand, the concept of development has been criticized as "a Eurocentric and hierarchic construct defining non-Western, non-modern, non-industrialized ways of life as inferior and in need of development".[29] In other words, given that the traditional donor camp is largely composed of former colonial powers, their engagements with the developing world and development cooperation efforts have been subjects of much postcolonial critique. A key postcolonial theme, in other words, concerns the process of decolonization currently taking place globally, which throws new light on the relationships between the hegemon and subaltern, colonizer and colonized.[30]

Having said that, while the impact and present-day legacies of the European colonial and development projects have been the focus of some academic inquiry, there has been an evident lack of relevant literature with regard to the Soviet modernization scheme and its many implications for the status quo in the post-socialist former Soviet states.

Hence, given the unique relationship between colonial past and development cooperation schemes in the current aid architecture, the discussion presented in this book turns the focus to Kazakhstan's ODA to analyze whether Kazakh aid offers an alternative to what have been conceptualized as OECD-DAC and SSC frameworks due to the peculiar nature of its emergence as an ODA provider.

Contribution to the Field

There are several reasons why Kazakhstan makes an interesting case to study. **First**, the Global North/Global South, developed/developing, the First World/the Third World countries lie at the core of theorization about North-South (N-S) and South-South (S-S) aid paradigms. It should be specifically stressed that the concept of SSC finds its roots in the struggle for independence of Asian and African countries during the 1940s and later in the Non-Aligned Movement (NAM). The idea of a common identity, equality and solidarity between less-developed countries; the defense of the sovereignty of newly independent states; and opposition to the "North" are the core elements of SSC.[31] As noted earlier, the "rise of the South" in recent decades has led to fundamental shifts in global development ideas, practices, norms and actors. Thus, existing literature is mainly concerned with "old"/Northern and "new"/Southern donors.

Building on the above discussion, however, this research argues that Kazakhstan does not fit either of these categories and in fact stands as an "outlier", falling outside any of these groups due to its historical experiences.

Kazakhstan (as well as other Soviet republics) was not an independent member of the global system at the time of the "First-Second-Third World" classification, and hence was not categorized as a "Third World" state when the term was first coined.

Some might argue that the dissolution of the Soviet communist bloc pushed the former Soviet socialist republics from the Second World to the Third World group. While we can find economic justifications for such categorization, this transition does not make much sense according to the political criterion of the Third World. In particular, the countries of the former Soviet bloc did not join the Non-Aligned Movement upon gaining their independence in the early 1990s. Instead, they were largely interested in adopting "development-oriented" policies and practices and were eagerly learning from the experience of the First World nations at least in the first years of independence.

Thus, the re-categorization of these states, including Kazakhstan, from the Second to the Third World countries, which some defined as "re-joining the Third World", can only be justified by the fact that, as the Soviet Union ceased to exist, post-communist countries experienced a decline in the level of development. However, this observation opens up a bigger debate regarding the meaning of the word "development", considering these nations' relatively high performance in education, human capital and other development indexes, which will be discussed in more detail in following chapters. Hence, while some labeled this transformation of the former socialist republics as their "re-joining" the Third World camp, it arguably would be more accurate to conceptualize the process as "de-development".

Kazakhstan, as a post-communist country, was committed to development, but not to reviving the ailing Third Worldism.[32] This study therefore finds the practice of incorporating Kazakhstan into the new/"Southern" donors group rather problematic.

Second, postcolonial theory has been applied to the former Western colonies that were represented as the Third World in the development discourse. Coined in the 1950s, the term "Third World" referred to the growing number of nonaligned nation states, which were reluctant to take sides in the Cold War.[33] Relatedly, development, thus, was criticized for being "an ideology that was born and refined in the North"[34] that promised "material affluence to decolonizing countries in Africa and Asia in order to prevent them from joining the communist camp and maintaining a colonial division of labor".[35]

As it was noted earlier, Kazakhstan has never been a part of the Third World group in its initial sense. In addition to that, prior to independence in 1991, Kazakhstan did not follow the path of Western modernization, but was a subject of Soviet modernization. So, while in the countries of Global South (some of which later became known as Southern donors) "the mental space in which people dream and act [was] occupied by Western imagery",[36] in Kazakhstan it was occupied by the "Soviet imagery". After all, the West and the USSR followed different paths of modernization. Therefore, the second point this research aims to highlight is the fact that there are some serious drawbacks in theoretical assumptions and conceptual tools that scholars in development studies should be uncomfortable with when applying them to the post-communist context.

This book argues that while development and postcolonial studies focus on the relationship between the former First World/"global North" and the Third World "global South", we know relatively little about the role and position of the former Soviet republics that have once been labeled as the Second World countries in the development aid landscape. This book aims to emphasize that postcolonial studies developed out of an entirely different range of historic and geo-historic experiences. Given the socio-political and cultural differences between Western and post-Soviet societies, we cannot assume that the methodological tools and theoretical perspectives developed in Western context are necessarily applicable to Kazakhstan. In fact, the unique experience of such countries as Kazakhstan and the inability of the Cold War terminology to convincingly and thoughtfully capture and conceptualize these experiences highlight the outdated nature of those concepts, which do not seem to be relevant in the present times.

Third, the observed phenomenon points at the general persistent invisibility of the post-Soviet space in social sciences. In the aftermath of the fall of the communist bloc, there was not much effort from Western researchers to continue to offer in-depth studies of the collapsed USSR. In fact, after the Cold War came to an end and the "enemy" was defeated, "the end of history" was announced.[37] As a result, except for the interest from transitologists, the post-Soviet world became largely ignored and overlooked.

This is especially true for Central Asia. Although many researchers acknowledge the importance of Central Asian studies, finding ways of keeping the field alive and turning it into a prospering research area remains a substantial obstacle.

Despite some noticeable progress in relevant scholarship, there are still many more unanswered questions, untested theories and untranslated evidence pertaining to various phenomena observed in this underexplored region. Central Asia's experience, both past and present, often challenges dominant intellectual paradigms and tends to be different from that of its neighbors, thus occupying a difficult place within disciplines. While some may find the current state of affairs to be an exciting opportunity to develop new, more-fitting intellectual paradigms, this enthusiasm is not always met in the relatively conservative academic environment.

This is not surprising, considering that for a long time, until very recently in fact, the production of knowledge has remained an exclusively Western affair.[38] Lander (1998, p. 71) adds that "the problem resides in the colonial imaginary from which Western social sciences constructed their interpretation of the world".

Recently, scholars started to raise questions about the absence of non-Western theories. Amitav Achary and Barry Buzan (2010) for instance introduced non-Western IR traditions, focusing on Asia, "because it has its own long history [...] and is quite distinct from that of the West". They claimed that "history matters" for international relations theorizing, because "even a short reflection on Western IRT quickly exposes that much of it is conspicuously drawn from the model provided by modern European history". They further added that "we are acutely aware that we are excluding the Middle East, whose history has an equal claim to standing as a distinctive source of IR". Following this logic, Central Asian history should also have immediate relevance to theoretical considerations. However, as practice shows, it is often a challenge to convince those outside of the field of Central Asian studies that the region matters.

Certain scholars dealing with Central Asia, of course, are concerned with how the material from Central Asia "can inform conceptual debates about order, knowledge, modernity, empire, religion and resources in the widest sense".[39] Sadly, there is currently a lack of effort on the part of Central Asian researchers to conceptualize their own experience and diverge from dominant discourses. In this way, local scholars continue to serve as informants, rather than producers of theory in a Western hegemony of knowledge production. When analyzing their past experiences or current circumstances, Central Asian scholars rarely move beyond the prisms of nostalgic Soviet myth or anti-Soviet idealization of the West.

What has been lacking, is intellectually independent critical discourse that would offer a body of knowledge reflecting local histories and experiences. Hence, it is vital that local knowledge and knowledge production are decolonized, and the self-colonizing syndrome, which currently dominates the space, is abandoned. It is important that Western and non-Western models are not simply acknowledged and re-applied to explain various phenomena in the local context but are thoroughly deconstructed and challenged by well-developed and relevant, original and vigorous local discourses about itself.

This is exactly where the broad theoretical interest and aim of this research come from. In the following chapters, the present research aims to demonstrate that Kazakhstan presents a challenge to the spatial matrices underpinning current postcolonial thinking, particularly the Global North/South distinction in current debate on development cooperation and the histories of colonialism.[40]

Notes

1. James, L., & Leake, E. (2015). *Decolonization and the Cold War* (1st ed.). Bloomsbury Academic.
2. Darwin, J. (1988). *Britain and decolonisation: The retreat from empire in the post-war world*. Macmillan.
3. Pieterse, J. N. (1991). Dilemmas of development discourse: The crisis of developmentalism and the comparative method. *Development and Change, 22*(1), 5–29. http://doi.org/10.1111/j.1467-7660.1991.tb00401.x.
4. Sachs, W. (1992). *The development dictionary: A guide to knowledge as power* (1st ed.). Zed Books.
5. Truman, H. (1949). *Inaugural Address of Harry S. Truman*. Speech. The Avalon Project. Documents in Law, History and Diplomacy. https://avalon.law.yale.edu/20th_century/truman.asp.
6. Sachs, W. (1992). *The development dictionary: A guide to knowledge as power* (1st ed.). Zed Books.
7. Macekura, S. (2013). The Point Four Program and U.S. international development policy. *Political Science Quarterly*, *128*(1), 127–160. www.jstor.org/stable/23563372.

8. Ryan, H. (1993). President Harry S. Truman's Inaugural Address. In H. Ryan, *The inaugural addresses of twentieth-century American presidents* (1st ed., pp. 141–152). Praeger Publishers.
9. Noguchi, M. (2005). Globalism and developmentalism. In C. Lapavitsas & M. Noguchi, *Beyond Market-Driven Development* (1st ed.). Routledge.
10. Escobar, A. (1995). *Encountering development: The making and unmaking of the Third World* (1st ed.). Princeton University Press.
11. Pieterse, J. N. (1991). Dilemmas of development discourse: The crisis of developmentalism and the comparative method. *Development and Change, 22*(1), 5–29. http://doi.org/10.1111/j.1467-7660.1991.tb00401.x.
12. Sachs, W. (1992). *The development dictionary: A guide to knowledge as power* (1st ed.). Zed Books.
13. Sachs, W. (1992). *The development dictionary: A guide to knowledge as power* (1st ed.). Zed Books; Escobar, A. (1995). *Encountering development: The making and unmaking of the Third World* (1st ed.). Princeton University Press.
14. Rapley, J. (2004). Development studies and the post-development critique. *Progress in Development Studies, 4*(4), 350–354. http://doi.org/10.1191/1464993404ps095pr.
15. Ziai, A. (2013). The discourse of "development" and why the concept should be abandoned. *Development in Practice, 23*(1), 123–136. http://doi.orgt/10.1080/09614524.2013.752792
16. Esteva (1987, p. 135).
17. Sachs, W. (1992). *The development dictionary: A guide to knowledge as power* (1st ed.). Zed Books.
18. Ziai, A. (2007). *Exploring post-development: Theory and practice*. Routledge.
19. James, L., & Leake, E. (2015). *Decolonization and the Cold War* (1st ed.). Bloomsbury Academic.
20. Smith, A., & Jeppesen, C. (2017). *Britain, France and the decolonization of Africa: Future imperfect?* (1st ed.). UCL Press.
21. Pieterse, J. N. (1991). Dilemmas of development discourse: The crisis of developmentalism and the comparative method. *Development and Change, 22*(1), 5–29.
22. Rapley, J. (2004). Development studies and the post-development critique. *Progress in Development Studies, 4*(4), 350–354.

23. Escobar, A. (1995). *Encountering development: The making and unmaking of the Third World* (1st ed.). Princeton University Press.
24. Ibid.
25. McEwan, C. (200). *Postcolonialism and development* (1st ed.). Routledge.
26. Noxolo, P. (2016). Postcolonial approaches to development. In J. Grugel & D. Hammett, *The Palgrave handbook of international development* (1st ed.). Palgrave Macmillan.
27. Hout, W. (2016). Classical approaches to development. In J. Grugel & D. Hammett, *The Palgrave handbook of international development* (1st ed.). Palgrave Macmillan.
28. Schuurman, F. J. (2000). Paradigms lost, paradigms regained? Development studies in the twenty-first century. *Third World Quarterly, 21*(1), 7–20. http://doi.org/10.1080/01436590013198.
29. Ziai, A. (2017). Post-development 25 years after the development dictionary. *Third World Quarterly, 38*(12), 2547–2558. http://doi.org/10.1080/01436597.2017.1383853.
30. Kapoor, I. (2008). *The postcolonial politics of development* (1st ed.). Routledge.
31. Bergamaschi et al. (2017).
32. Ma, S. (1998). Third World studies, development studies and post-communist studies: Definitions, distance and dynamism. *Third World Quarterly, 19*(3), 339–356.
33. Berger, M. (1994). The end of the 'Third World'? *Third World Quarterly, 15*(2), 257–275. Retrieved March 14, 2020, from www.jstor.org/stable/3993146.
34. Rahnema, M. (1997) Introduction. In M. Rahnema & V. Bawtree (Eds.), *The post-development reader*. Zed Books.
35. Ziai, A. (2017). Post-development 25 years after the development dictionary. *Third World Quarterly, 38*(12), 2547–2558.
36. Sachs, W. (1992). *The development dictionary: A guide to knowledge as power* (1st ed.). Zed Books; Escobar, A. (1995). *Encountering development: The making and unmaking of the Third World* (1st ed.). Princeton University Press.
37. Fukuyama, F. (1992). *The end of history and the last man*. Free Press.
38. Acharya, A., & Buzan, B. (2010). *Non-Western international relations theory: Perspectives on and beyond Asia* (1st ed.). Routledge.

39. Dubuisson, E. (2017). *Reflections on a workshop "The future of Central Asian studies"*. [Blog] http://thecessblog.com/2017/10/reflections-on-a-workshop-the-future-of-central-asian-studies/.
40. Raghuram, P., Noxolo, P., & Madge, C. (2013). Rising Asia and postcolonial geography. *Singapore Journal of Tropical Geography, 35*(1), 119–135. http://doi.org/10.1111/sjtg.12045.

CHAPTER 3

The "Development" Paradigm: Official Development Assistance and DAC

Abstract This chapter provides a brief overview of the history of foreign aid, as well as the main narratives that dominate the literature on development and humanitarian aid provision. The chapter also sheds light on the existing studies dedicated to Kazakh aid and explains how the Kazakh donorship has been approached up until now.

Keywords Organization for Economic Cooperation and Development (OECD) · Development Assistance Committee (DAC) · Foreign aid · KazAID · Kazakh aid · Official Development Assistance (ODA) · Development aid

Defining what foreign aid means and categorizing different types of aid remains a tricky and challenging endeavor. There exist various studies that aim to describe and conceptualize foreign aid, as well as shed light on its organization, function and effect. As put by Hattori (2001), however, despite existing disagreements on the precise definition of foreign aid and what it does, experts mostly agree that "foreign aid consists of material goods or services that are owned or controlled by donors, the allocation of which may vary according to their purposes and interests".[1] Aid, in general, is broadly divided into development and humanitarian assistance.

N. Insebayeva, *Modernity, Development and Decolonization of Knowledge in Central Asia*, Politics and History in Central Asia,
https://doi.org/10.1007/978-981-16-5117-5_3

There are a number of important distinctions between humanitarian aid, which is designed to achieve immediate (short-term) humanitarian imperatives, and development aid, which centers on the long-term development goals. The European Union defines the former as efforts aimed at "saving people's lives in crisis situations and addressing their basic needs by providing food, shelter or medical care in conflicts or after natural disasters".[2] Foreign aid experts have first detected a significant funding gap between these two types of international assistance in the 1990s—the fact that drew significant scholarly attention to the discussion of the humanitarian-development aid nexus. However, a growing number of studies point at the fact that the gap between the two concepts is closing as the distinction between the two becomes less and less clear.

The dominant definition of development aid is the one proposed by the Development Assistance Committee (DAC) within the Organization for Economic Cooperation and Development (OECD), which was initially suggested in 1969 and tightened in 1972.[3] According to the OECD, foreign aid in the form of Official Development Assistance (ODA) is defined as "those flows to countries and territories in the DAC List of ODA Recipients and to multilateral institutions which are:

i. provided by official agencies, including state and local governments, or by their executive agencies; and
ii. each transaction of which:
    (a) is administered with the promotion of the economic development and welfare of developing countries as its main objective; and
    (b) is concessional in character and conveys a grant element of at least 25 per cent (calculated at a rate of discount of 10 per cent)".[4]

All states and territories that are eligible for receiving ODA are included in the DAC list of aid recipients, which was designed to collect data for statistical purposes. It is important to note that the OECD and DAC membership does not affect actors' chances to be featured in the list, which gets revised every three years, with new recipients added and some removed based on their ability to reach high-income status within a given period of time. In this light, providing assistance to low- and middle-income countries for the purpose of achieving economic development and welfare as the main objective is, perhaps, the most important criteria for aid to qualify as ODA.

As to what types of activities can be classified as ODA, the DAC has spent a great amount of time revising and refining the detailed ODA reporting rules in order to "ensure fidelity to the definition and the greatest possible consistency among donors" (ibid.). As such, members have reached an agreement in regard to ODA eligibility, i.e., what is included in the official international foreign aid. In particular, military aid in the form of provision of military equipment and services, anti-terrorism activities, as well as the enforcement aspect of peacekeeping, especially the ones carried out outside of the UN-approved and UN-administered framework, cannot be reported as ODA.[5] Other areas included in the ODA reporting, with varying degrees of limitations imposed, are civil police work, social and cultural programs, assistance to refugees, nuclear energy and research (ibid.). Thus, the concept of ODA is not designed to track private donations and can be highly controversial due to the complexity associated with distinguishing various contributions by type.

Development assistance can take many forms and can be distributed through different mechanisms. Governments typically employ bilateral and multilateral aid channels to assist recipient states in achieving their developmental objectives. A significant portion of the world's foreign aid is distributed via multilateral methods; in particular, funds are transferred to such international organizations as the United Nations, the World Bank, the International Monetary Fund and others. Within this system, international institutions rely on finances coming from international capital markets and annual contributions made by their member-countries. Contrary to this method of aid delivery, bilateral assistance strictly refers to the type of aid that is distributed from one government to another. In Kazakhstan's case, the primary institution responsible for the distribution of Kazakh aid is the Ministry of Foreign Affairs of the Republic of Kazakhstan. According to the OECD report, in 2017, 25.5% of Kazakhstan's gross Official Development Assistance was provided bilaterally, while its other donor commitments were allocated through multilateral organizations.[6] The type of aid that is often preferred by donor- and recipient countries alike is called project aid. The term refers to the kind of development assistance where funds are used to finance a specific purpose with visible outputs (e.g., road construction). Donors and recipients tend to favor this type of aid over others due to the tangible results it is designed to produce that align with economic and political interests of all actors involved.[7]

In contrast to project aid, program aid represents the form of assistance that is not aimed at specific tangible or visible targets. It is mostly intended to assist recipient states in achieving broader policy objectives. Program aid is often accompanied by a list of conditions, which aid recipients must meet before any fund allocation is made. A good example of program aid is debt relief packages provided by the International Monetary Fund (IMF) or the World Bank. Within this framework, disbursements are approved only in case the recipient country is able to demonstrate that it has significantly reduced its public sector spending.

Technical assistance is aid that comes in the form of expertise and equipment required to promote development through providing training to local specialists. This human capital-oriented type of aid is different from other forms of assistance in that although money is used to cover operating costs, it does not involve direct financial support, such as outright grants and loans. There exist other kinds of assistance that include food, medical and disaster aid.[8]

Origins of Foreign Aid

While the concept and various forms of aid-giving in its broader sense have been argued to date all the way back to pre-colonial times,[9] a general consensus in the foreign aid literature has been to conceptualize it as an essential foreign policy tool used by developed countries to assist less developed countries in achieving a variety of different goals in the aftermath of World War II.[10] In fact, much of foreign aid scholarship argues that modern understanding of development assistance has its origins in the Cold War and can be broadly defined as a product of systemic ideological confrontation between the Soviet Union and Western powers.[11] In other words, it has been widely accepted that the 45-year period of intensive rivalry between communism and capitalism was the years when foreign aid in its present-day sense became an important feature of international politics.[12]

Development aid as we know it today did not start as an attempt to extend assistance aimed at achieving long-term development objectives in the impoverished states; rather, it was commenced as an initiative designed to facilitate short-term economic recovery of Western Europe in the post-war period.[13] More specifically, the Marshall Plan introduced by the USA in 1948 to assist Western Europe is argued to be the first large-scale foreign aid initiative used to simultaneously promote foreign policy interests of the donor while helping Europe rebuild.[14] Fanned by the growing threat of the spread of communism in Europe and the rapidly declining European economies, President Truman and Secretary of State George Marshall have initially devised an economic stimulus program aimed at all European states, including the Soviet Union, Germany and the Eastern bloc.[15] However, as explained by Roberts (1994), the Soviet Union withdrew from the initially welcomed[16] US-led initiative due to its concerns over the coordinated multilateral nature of the program, which could potentially harm Soviet influence over Eastern Europe.

As such, the Marshall Plan, which sought to halt the spread of communism and strengthen democracy in Western Europe, was followed by the aforementioned Truman's Point Four Program, which targeted Greece and Turkey due to the growing communist movements and the outbreak of civil wars in those states.[17] The US government believed that the necessity for the program stemmed from the potential risk of destabilization of the Middle East if Greece and Turkey fell to communism.[18]

The successful implementation of these initiatives has produced important long-term economic, political and socio-cultural impacts both in the States and abroad. In particular, the plan has established and fostered American-style capitalist market economies and restored democratic rule throughout Western Europe, which has ultimately affected the balance of power in Europe.[19] Following this phase in American foreign policy, the USA and its Western allies continued to utilize foreign aid as an important tool of Western diplomacy in approaching the newly independent countries in Asia and Africa freed from colonial rule.[20]

Given the clear foreign policy objectives of the Marshall Plan, it was rejected by the USSR, which instead announced its own project to restore the war-torn Europe (specifically its Eastern part, which the Soviet Union had control over) titled the Molotov Plan.[21] More specifically, the Soviet regime believed the American initiative to be an anti-communist effort to advance democracy and free-market economy, which could undermine the communist influence and stability in the Eastern bloc.[22] Thus, the Marshall Plan and its aftermath are believed by many experts to have played a key role in the origin and development of the Cold War.[23]

The so-called Molotov Plan involved a series of bilateral trade agreements between the Eastern European states and the USSR that were designed to assist the former to achieve economic development. One of the first steps in the plan was the establishment of the Communist Information Bureau (kominformbyuro) in 1947.[24] According to Mosley (1987), it was not until the second half of the 1950s when the Soviet Union became a significant international aid provider. Similarly, White (1974) reports that in the late 1950s rich countries, in particular, those of North America and Europe, started to expand the coverage of their aid programs with an increasing number of countries becoming recipients of Western aid.[25] Thus, the aid system developed amidst and partly as a result of the Cold War was highly dual in nature with the Western bloc establishing aid programs aimed at democracy and market economy promotion and the USSR responding with initiatives designed to extend communism.[26]

Meanwhile, in 1961, following the start of the OECD's operation, it passed a Ministerial Resolution that established the DAC, i.e., the largest donors' club, as a part of the organization. The Committee was based on the previously founded Development Assistance Group (DAG)—a consultation forum for foreign aid providers to discuss assistance strategies to help developing countries. The original DAG members included Belgium, Canada, France, Germany, Italy, Portugal, the United Kingdom, the USA, Japan, the Netherlands and the Commission of the European Economic Community.[27]

In 1958, the World Council of Churches presented the international community with a motion calling on the donor countries to transfer 1% of their income to the developing states. By 1968, after a long process of refining, all DAC members had subscribed to the suggested target. However, due to some drawbacks of the originally set goal including the main challenge of governments being unable to predict, control and/or compensate for private flows, the target was revised; and, in 1969, the Pearson Commission proposed the ODA target to be set at 0.7% of gross national product (GNP), which was to be reached by 1975.[28] The proposal was later formalized by the United Nations (UN) General Assembly, which included the target in a Resolution on October 24, 1970. The Resolution had been adopted by the majority of DAC donors with the exception of Switzerland, which did not become a member of the UN until 2002, and the USA, which despite agreeing with the general aims of the Resolution, did not subscribe to any timetables or targets. An important note is that the target was later revised with GNP being replaced by an equivalent concept, gross national income (GNI) (ibid.).

Despite subscribing to the target, only six DAC countries (Norway—1.05%, Sweden—1.04%, Luxembourg—0.95%, Denmark—0.85%, the Netherlands—0.75% and the United Kingdom—0.7%) were able to meet the so-called 0.7 target in 2015.[29] Interestingly enough, while the unwillingness of some donors to make an effort to offer more development assistance to less developed national economies makes them the target of worldwide criticism, other aid providers get criticized for their "overspending" on foreign aid as, for example, in the case of the United Kingdom (ibid.). Thus, the question of whether foreign aid does, in fact, boost development in the recipient countries is a subject of a heated debate. While the effectiveness of aid in helping the recipients to achieve certain objectives has been a hotly contested issue, it is hard to argue with the observation that aid has always had some geopolitical ramifications.[30] Many experts call for more aid, whereas others argue that the system of aid allocation should be changed in order to facilitate growth and development in the recipient countries. The latter camp consists of many diverse views, which generally seems to insist that it is not only how much aid we provide that determines the success or failure of a particular assistance initiative, but also the who, whom, when, where and how that matter the most. In other words, the interests of donors and recipients, as well as the aid allocation patterns themselves, play a crucial role in actors' ability to achieve the officially desirable results.

Literature on Kazakh Aid: How It Has Been Approached So Far

Although Kazakhstan has a long-standing record of providing emergency relief and humanitarian aid to foreign countries (reportedly roughly $100 million as of 2013),[31] the decision to establish a permanent structure to oversee its development assistance to partner countries has provoked a heated debate on the rationale behind the initiative.[32] However, the current discussion in the literature is limited to rationalist explanations for the objectives Kazakhstan might wish to pursue through establishing its aid agency. A common thread in the existing studies on Kazakh aid is that Kazakhstan deploys foreign aid as a foreign policy tool in pursuit of its economic, political and diplomatic objectives. It is widely assumed that Kazakhstan aims to contribute to the stabilization of the socioeconomic and political situation in its partner countries through foreign aid allocations in order to create "a belt of good neighborhood" along its borders.[33] One of the explanations of Kazakhstan's motivation to give a hand to the neighboring states is that by reducing and eliminating problems that have arisen from underdevelopment in neighboring countries (e.g., illegal migration flows, drug trafficking and other forms of crimes, including terrorism and extremism), Kazakhstan aims to prevent penetration of these problems inside its own state.[34]

Furthermore, it has been argued that Kazakhstan's ODA is ultimately connected to the increasing "redefinition of power balances and spheres of influence" in the region.[35] That is, Kazakhstan with the official status of a state-donor can use its ODA for "hard power" economic and political leverage during negotiation processes with partner countries in its neighborhood (i.e., potential or current Kazakh aid recipients). This could possibly provide the country with an additional mechanism of influence and increase its bargaining power opposite its foreign aid dependents. In other words, from this perspective, aid is assessed as an investment for future returns, because it is determined by pragmatic calculations of economic and/or geostrategic nature.

Another study that aimed to shed light on the motivations driving the creation of KazAID argues that the rationale behind the establishment of a national system of ODA is not limited to material interests, and there is also a soft power dimension to it.[36] Some scholars conceptualize foreign aid "as solidarity", arguing that "with the economic development and growth of the international prestige of the country, the responsibility of Kazakhstan for ensuring international and regional security and stability increases".[37]

Even though all these explanations might be plausible, they engender more questions than answers. For instance, while there seem to be political benefits to launching KazAID, it might be challenging for Kazakhstan from an economic standpoint. More specifically, within the last few years, Kazakhstan's economy has shrunk significantly under the conditions of a deepening economic crisis.[38] Kazakhstan experienced one of the most major economic shocks back in 2008 and was struck again after a stunning threefold fall in oil prices in 2014–2016. The slowdown in economic performance in Kazakhstan's two largest trading partners—Russia and China—has added to the mix, leading to a dramatic currency collapse. Kazakh Tenge dropped from 151KZT per dollar in January 2013 to 357KZT per dollar in January 2016. In 2015, Kazakhstan was even predicted to be one of the ten world's worst performers in terms of economic growth as the host of one of the worst performing currencies.[39]

On top of that, it can be argued that Kazakhstan does not have a lot of capital to use for foreign aid purposes. In 2015, Kazakhstan took a loan amounting to $1 billion from the Asian Development Bank to continue governmental programs that aim to stabilize the economy following the adoption of free-floating exchange rate and increasing inflation[40] and $40 million from the World Bank to help enhance competitiveness and management capacity of small and medium-sized enterprises in the country.[41] In 2016, Kazakhstan reached an agreement with the International Bank for Reconstruction and Development to loan $100 million for stimulating new jobs creation.[42] That is, the external debt of Kazakhstan increased to $165.3 billion in 2016 from $157.1 billion in 2014.[43]

The argument of soft power boosting[44] cannot fully explain Kazakhstan's foreign aid policy as well. Whereas it is understandable that Kazakhstan might wish to achieve "external legitimization as a cooperative, developed and reliable actor on the international stage",[45] it does not clearly explain the motives of Kazakhstan's decision to embark upon providing aid given the economic and political context within the country. Not only does the country continue to experience economic hardships, but also the crisis of legitimacy of the regime, which can be observed from the growing discontent among the population.[46] For years, the legitimacy of the current regime rested on the hierarchy of priorities between the political authorities and the population: state sovereignty, social stability and economic development.[47] However, lately, the regime's successful legitimacy has been threatened by the current economic situation. According to the World Bank national accounts data (2016), Kazakhstan's GDP growth indicator decreased from 6 in 2013 to 4.2 in 2014 (almost twice) and has been dropping ever since. The national budget was cut by $3.3 billion by non-priority investments and delaying increases in public salaries. Budget cuts were even partially offset by an additional $1.9 billion from the National Fund. Nevertheless, in 2014, Kazakhstan's net ODA amounted for $33 million compared to $8 million in 2013—an increase of 292% in real terms—and has been expanded even further in 2015 ($43 million) (ODA key statistics, 2016).

All of these shortcomings aside, the existing literature on Kazakh aid leaves another important question out of the scope of their analysis. While the studies aim to address the question "why" and focus on describing the motivations behind Kazakh aid, they ignore the question "how" and do not offer explanations for what Kazakhstan's identity as a donor is and how exactly it has been shaped. The following chapters will address these questions in detail.

Notes

1. Hattori, T. (2001). Re-conceptualizing foreign aid. *Review of International Political Economy, 8*(4), 633–660. http://dx.doi.org/10.1080/09692290110077610.
2. EU development aid. (2015). Retrieved from the Official Website of the European Union. https://europa.eu/eyd2015/en/content/eu-development-aid.
3. Official development assistance—Definition and coverage. (n.d.) http://www.oecd.org/dac/stats/officialdevelopmentassistancedefinitionandcoverage.htm#Definition.
4. Ibid.
5. Is it ODA? (2008). *OECD Factsheet.* http://www.oecd.org/dac/stats/34086975.pdf.
6. OECD. (2019). Kazakhstan. In *Development Co-operation Profiles.* OECD Publishing.
7. Israel (1987).
8. Tisch, S., & Wallace, M. (1994). Dilemmas of development assistance: The what, why and who of Foreign Aid; Hoy, P. (1997). Players and Issues in International Aid.
9. Cohen, R. (2001). The great tradition: The spread of diplomacy in the ancient world. *Diplomacy and Statecraft, 12*(1), 23–38.
10. Lancaster, C. (2007). *Foreign Aid: Diplomacy, development, domestic politics.* University of Chicago Press; Palmer, G., Wohlander, S. B., & Morgan, T. C. (2002). Give or take: Foreign aid and foreign policy substitutability. *Journal of Peace Research, 39*(1), 5–26. http://www.jstor.org/stable/425255; Qian, N. (2014). *Making progress on foreign aid* (Annual Review of Economics 3).
11. Griffin, K. (1996). Foreign Aid after the Cold War. In *Studies in Globalization and Economic Transitions.* Palgrave Macmillan.
12. Mosley, P. (1987). *Foreign Aid: Its defense and reform.* University Press of Kentucky.
13. Griffin, K. (1996). Foreign Aid after the Cold War. In *Studies in Globalization and Economic Transitions.* Palgrave Macmillan.

14. Milner, H., & Tingley, D. H. (2013). Introduction to geopolitics of foreign aid. In *Geopolitics of Foreign Aid.* Edward Elgar.
15. Weissman, A. D. (2013). Pivotal politics—The Marshall Plan: A turning point in foreign aid and the struggle for democracy. *The History Teacher, 47*(1), 111–129.
16. Although the Soviet elites were willing to participate in negotiations over the initiative and were at the time driven by the inspiration to cooperate with the West, one should be careful not to read the Soviet original embrace of the Marshall Plan talks as anything more than its refusal to dismiss the proposal before carefully assessing its goals and potential risks for the USSR (see Roberts, 1994).
17. President Truman's Message to Congress, March 12, 1947, Document 171, 80th Congress, 1st Session, Records of the US House of Representatives, record group 233, National Archives.
18. US Department of State, "Milestones: 1945–1952," Office of the Historian, Bureau of Public Affairs, 2.
19. Hitchcock, W. I. (2013). The Marshall Plan and the creation of the West. In M. P. Leffler (Ed.), *The Cambridge history of the Cold War* (pp. 154–174). Cambridge University Press.
20. Griffin, K. (1996). Foreign Aid after the Cold War. In *Studies in globalization and economic transitions.* Palgrave Macmillan.
21. Cromwell, W. C. (1979). The Marshall non-plan, congress and the Soviet Union. *The Western Political Quarterly, 32*(4), 422–443.
22. Weissman, A. D. (2013). Pivotal politics—The Marshall Plan: A turning point in foreign aid and the struggle for democracy. *The History Teacher, 47*(1), 111–129.
23. Roberts, G. (1994). Moscow and the Marshall plan: Politics, ideology and the onset of the Cold War, 1947. *Europe-Asia Studies, 46*(8), 1371–1386.
24. Berger, M. (1948). How the Molotov Plan works. *The Antioch Review, 8*(1), 17–25.
25. White, J. (1974). *The politics of foreign aid.* London: Bodley Head.
26. Milner, H., & Tingley, D. H. (2013). Introduction to geopolitics of foreign aid. In *Geopolitics of Foreign Aid.* Edward Elgar.
27. The DAC: 50 years, 50 highlights (2010).
28. History of the 0.7% ODA target. (2002). *DAC Journal, 3*(4), 9–11.

29. Official Development Assistance. (2016). *Issue Brief Series*; Quinn, B. (2017, January 4). UK among six countries to hit 0.7% UN aid spending target. *The Guardian*.
30. Milner, H., & Tingley, D. H. (2013). Introduction to geopolitics of foreign aid. In *Geopolitics of Foreign Aid*. Edward Elgar.
31. Ukaz Prezidenta. (2013, April 9). Kontseptsiya Respubliki Kazakhstan v sfere ofictsial'noi pomoshchi razvitiyu.
32. OCHA. (2013). *Regionalniy obzor gumanitarnogo finansirovania—Kavkaz i Tsentral'naia Azia* (No. 8 and No. 9).
33. Mirzayan, G. (2014). Kazakhstan formiruet poyas dobrososedstva. *Expert*.
34. Ibid.
35. De Cordier, B. (2014). Kazakhstan and Azerbaijan as donors of humanitarian aid: Has the diversification of aid channels and donors reached Southern Eurasia? *Central Asia and the Caucasus, 15*(4).
36. Malyshev, D., & Bainazarova, E. (2016). Russia and Kazakhstan: Mutually different interests for regional leadership. In H. Rytövuori-Apunen (Ed.), *The regional security puzzle around Afghanistan: Bordering practices in Central Asia and beyond* (pp. 243–270).
37. Aitmukhambetov and Ardabayeva (2014).
38. Kapparov, K. (2016). *Invisible pubic debt: The case of Kazakhstan* (CAP Papers 171).
39. Kamalova, G. (2015, July 14). Kazakhstan in 10 world's worst performers in economy: Bloomberg. *Tengrinews;* Wallace, P. (2016, August 23). *World's worst currency slump gleaning rewards for Nigeria*. Bloomberg.
40. ADB $1 Billion loan to help Kazakhstan counter economic slowdown (2015).
41. World Bank to help Kazakhstan SMEs become more competitive (2015).
42. Kazakhstan ratifies loan agreement with IBRD. (2016). *Kazinform*.
43. Trading Economics. (2016). *Kazakhstan Gross External Debt 1995–2017*.
44. De Cordier, B. (2014). Kazakhstan and Azerbaijan as donors of humanitarian aid: Has the diversification of aid channels and

donors reached Southern Eurasia? *Central Asia And The Caucasus, 15*(4); Malyshev, D., & Bainazarova, E. (2016). Russia and Kazakhstan: Mutually different interests for regional leadership. In H. Rytövuori-Apunen (Ed.), *The regional security puzzle around Afghanistan: Bordering practices in Central Asia and beyond* (pp. 243–270).

45. Posega, P. (2015). Kazakhstan beyond Borat. *Modern Diplomacy*.
46. Abdurasulov, A. (2016, May 23). Razgon protestov v Kazakhstane: rasskazy ochevidcev. *BBC*; Pannier, B. (2016, May 22). The reasons Kazakhs are protesting. *Radio Liberty*.
47. Laruelle, M. (2015, May 1). The power of soft power in Kazakhstan. *The Washington Post*.

CHAPTER 4

Kazakhstan as a Humanitarian Aid Donor

Abstract This chapter explores the activities of Kazakhstan as an aid provider. Having a long-standing record of offering emergency relief and humanitarian aid to foreign countries, Kazakhstan entered the emerging donors' camp in 2013 and was quick to dramatically increase its ODA budget over the years to come. The chapter discusses the constructed aid modality and highlights the main features and characteristics of Kazakhstan's ODA system. It starts with providing an overview of Kazakhstan's activities as a humanitarian aid donor and moves to the section on the adoption of relevant legislation pertaining to official development assistance.

Keywords Humanitarian aid · Development aid partner · UNDP · Central Asia · Law drafting · Domestic context

Many emerging aid providers have had track records of rendering assistance long before obtaining the official status of a "development aid donor country". Kazakhstan, for example, has provided aid to less developed countries (and those in need) since the early years of its independence.[1] In fact, according to Vladimir Bozhko, who served as the

N. Insebayeva, *Modernity, Development and Decolonization of Knowledge in Central Asia*, Politics and History in Central Asia,
https://doi.org/10.1007/978-981-16-5117-5_4

Table 4.1 Top donors in 2010 ranked by total humanitarian aid

	Biggest donors in 2010 (US$m)		*Most generous countries in 2010 (% GNI)*	
1	United States	4871	Sweden	0.15%
2	EU Institutions	1658	Luxembourg	0.14%
3	United Kingdom	943	Gambia	0.13%
4	Germany	744	Norway	0.11%
5	Sweden	690	Denmark	0.08%
6	Japan	642	Ireland	0,07%
7	Canada	550	Fin Land	0.07%
8	Spain	496	Saudi Arabia	0.06%
9	Norway	470	Netherlands	0.06%
10	Netherlands	459	Belgium	0.05%
11	France	435	Guyana	0.05%
12	Australia	390	United Kingdom	0.04%
13	Italy	283	UAE	0.04%
14	Denmark	259	Switzerland	0.04%
15	Saudi Arabia	256	Spain	0.04%
16	Belgium	227	Canada	0.04%
17	Switzerland	211	United States	0.03%
18	Finland	167	Australia	0.03%
19	Ireland	128	New Zealand	0.02%
20	UAE	114	Germany	0.02%
21	Austria	65	DRC	0.02%
22	Turkey	61	Timor-Leste	0.02%
23	Luxembourg	54	Kazakhstan	0.02%
24	Russian Federation	40	Equatorial Guinea	0.02%
25	Greece	39	Austria	0.02%
26	China	38	France	0.02%
27	India	37	Saint Lucia	0.02%
28	New Zealand	31	Saint Vincent and the Grenadines	0.01%
29	Brazil	29	Italy	0.01%
30	Kazakhstan	25	Grenada	0.01%

Source Global Humanitarian Assistance Report, 2012

Vice-Chairman of the Mazhilis, Kazakhstan has over the years provided over KZT 10 billion in humanitarian aid to foreign countries.[2]

The 2010 Global Humanitarian Assistance (GHA) report, which ranks non-DAC donors by total humanitarian aid provided in 2000–2009, put Kazakhstan on the 16th place in the list.[3] Interestingly, Kazakhstan was among top ten humanitarian aid providers in 2008, which significantly exceeded its previous and subsequent contributions (Table 4.1). Although

Kazakhstan's contribution can hardly be compared to the shares of the top five donors in the list, such a trend is of particular interest within the scope of this study. According to the 2012 GHA report, Kazakhstan made it to the top 30 largest government contributors of humanitarian aid in 2010, which included both DAC and non-DAC donors. Most importantly, it was called one of the most generous countries with its contribution amounting to 0.02% of the state's GNI that year, the rate, which was also provided by such developed economies as Austria and France.

The range of Kazakhstan's humanitarian activities was quite broad with the country engaging with the states all over the globe. For instance, in 2012, Kazakhstan sent the governments of Jordan and Lebanon US$400,000 through the Organization of Islamic Cooperation to be spent on humanitarian aid for Syrians in refugee camps.[4] 3 years later, in 2015, the country rendered over US$330,000 in medical and food aid to assist Syrian refugees based at the Turkish-Syrian border.[5]

In 2017, following President Nazarbayev's order, Kazakhstan sent about 500 tons of food aid to Syria.[6] Notably, then-Ambassador of Kazakhstan to Jordan Azamat Berdybai, who represented Kazakhstan at the meeting with the Syrian delegation, made sure to emphasize that "Kazakhstan backs the measures launched by the international community and the actions of the Syrian authorities and the opposition aimed at speedy ceasefire and determining the political future of Syria by means of dialogue and reconciliation".[7]

Moreover, Kazakhstan appeared on the list of the United Nations Office for the Coordination of Humanitarian Affairs (UN OCHA) donors in 2013 (US$99,970) and 2014 (US$50,000).[8] The organization also features Kazakhstan as one of the largest providers of humanitarian aid in the ROCCA region (Caucasus, Central Asia and Ukraine).[9] Interestingly, according to the 2016 GHA Report, states outside of the OECD-DAC group amounted for 70% of all direct humanitarian assistance provided to the affected governments, with Kazakhstan (U$8 million) being among the top three contributors alongside Saudi Arabia (US$121 million) and the United Arab Emirates (US$34 million).

Finally, Kazakhstan has a history of contributing to the development of one of the major aid recipients—the neighboring Afghanistan, specifically through the provision of wheat, construction of roads, hospitals and schools,[10] technical assistance and scholarship grants for Afghan students.[11] The latter show that Kazakhstan's involvement in the region

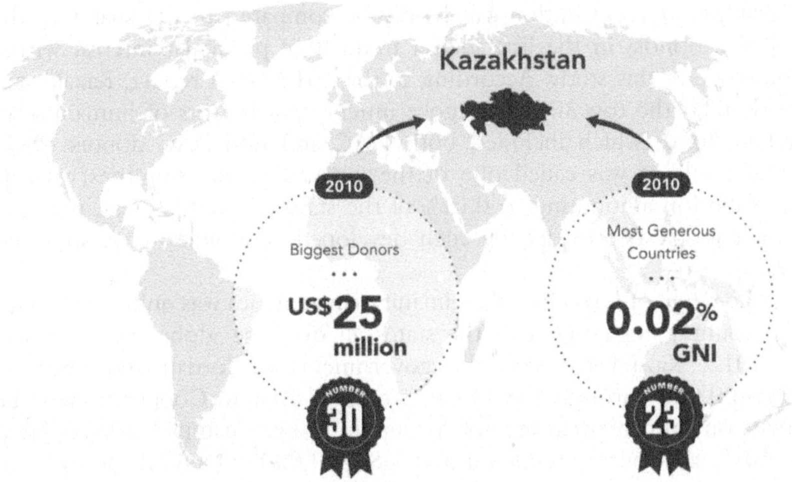

Fig. 4.1 Kazakhstan's ranking in total humanitarian aid (Author's compilation)

has not been limited to humanitarian aid and relief, but that the state has also been pursuing some developmental goals in the target recipients. President Nazarbayev has explained Kazakhstan's engagement with the state by emphasizing the growing global importance of the Central Asian region, which he believed no longer needed to be associated with conflicts and political instability. Nazarbayev stated that the main goal of the efforts of the states involved in the region, including Kazakhstan, should, thus, be economic development of the region and not achievement of local military objectives.[12] In this light, Kazakhstan's education initiative, according to Nazarbayev, was specifically designed to address these challenges in the country (ibid.). The more people covered by the initiative, the less the number of potential recruits for various terrorist groups. Thus, the Kazakhstani President called for other international aid providers to engage in economic development-oriented aid strategies in Afghanistan (Fig. 4.1).

Kazakhstan as a Development Aid Partner

In April 2013, Kazakhstan presented the ODA Concept of the Republic of Kazakhstan—the document ought to set the roadmap of the state's development aid initiative. The following year, in December 2014, the country launched its development aid program—the Kazakhstan Agency for International Development (KazAID), which officially made it the first foreign aid donor country from the Central Asian region. The Kazakh national system of ODA was established under the Ministry of Foreign Affairs (MFA) of Kazakhstan with the operating budget of 0.01% of GDP ($15–22 million in 2012–2016) for the purpose of providing development assistance primarily to the countries in its immediate neighborhood.

In the published Foreign Policy Concept for 2014–2020 of the Republic of Kazakhstan (2014), it is stated that "Kazakhstan has entered the third decade of its independence as an established and stable state with a dynamically developing economy and clearly set foreign policy priorities". The Foreign policy concept, which was created in line with the Address of the President of the Republic of Kazakhstan Nursultan Nazarbayev, emphasized the state's aspiration to contribute to the development of the international community through various cooperative efforts. It is worth noting that in 2013 Kazakhstan made a contribution to the Asian Development Bank amounting to five million dollars, which marked the start of its transition from a recipient of ADB's assistance to the first Central Asian donor of the organization.[13] Kazakhstan's aspiration of becoming an official ADB's partner, according to then-Prime Minister of the Republic of Kazakhstan Serik Akhmetov, was expected to secure the state's seat the "decision-making" table in the Bank and would allow for a deeper involvement of the state in the development-related issues in the Asian region.[14]

In 2014, the government also passed the Law of the Republic of Kazakhstan on Official Development Assistance. As the Kazakh governmental officials explained during interviews, after it has been decided that Kazakhstan shall adopt appropriate aid mechanisms to coordinate its aid contributions abroad, the government put significant resources into studying other countries' experiences as ODA providers and deepening international cooperation through building meaningful partnerships with key donors and international development institutions. Kazakhstani experts have studied the expertise of such international cooperation agencies as those of the USA (USAID), Germany (GIZ), Sweden (SIDA), Spain (AECID), Japan (JICA), Slovakia (SlovakAid), Czech Republic (CzDA) and South Korea (KOICA).[15]

As part of this process, on May 21, 2015, the Ministry of Foreign Affairs held a panel session titled "Kazakhstan ODA system. ODA Needs and Challenges Today and Tomorrow" at the VIII Astana Economic

Forum. During the discussion, the government representatives presented the interim results of Kazakhstan's efforts in creating its own national ODA system. Moreover, the panelists shared their insights on the prospects of potential multilateral and bilateral cooperation between Kazakhstan and various international organizations and foreign aid donors for the purpose of promoting international development.[16]

At the present time, the main objectives of the relevant government bodies responsible for the formation of the Kazakhstani ODA system are (1) ensuring institutionalization of ODA activities and creation of the national ODA operator—KazAID; (2) development of domestic expertise in the sphere of ODA; and (3) further development and promotion of cooperation with international development institutions and foreign aid donors.[17]

Given the importance of Kazakhstan's participation in global dialogue and ODA coordination, establishing and deepening cooperation with the OECD-DAC, a globally recognized club of donor countries, was proclaimed to be one of the main priority directions in the formation of the Kazakhstani ODA system. As such, taking into account the general course toward rapprochement with the OECD, after a series of bilateral consultation between DAC and Kazakhstani government, in 2015 Kazakhstan was granted the official status of Invitee to DAC. This status gives the country an opportunity to attend all public meetings and meetings sponsored by the Committee. In other words, a country-invitee gets directly involved in the global dialogue and aid coordination process without any financial, legal or other obligations. Since 2015, Kazakhstan has participated in multiple DAC-led meetings.[18]

As of 2019, as one of the conditions of the received status, the Ministry of Foreign Affairs of the Republic of Kazakhstan responsible for interaction with this structural unit of the OECD has submitted six aggregated statistical reports to the DAC. The documents contain government-collected information on the official development assistance provided by the Republic of Kazakhstan to foreign countries in the period 2013–2018. According to the reports provided to the author by MFA, the total amount of Kazakhstan's bilateral and multilateral development and humanitarian assistance was US$20.1 million in 2013, US$46.4 million in 2014, US$54.1 million in 2015, US$38 million in 2016, US$43.3 million in 2017 and US$54.9 million in 2018. As it is stated in the governmental report, the inclusion of this data in the official DAC reports signifies official recognition of Kazakhstan's donor activities by the international community. This, in turn, is said to significantly strengthen Kazakhstan's position on the global arena and influence potential political and image dividends the country can expect from engaging in this type of activity.[19]

An important part in the establishment of Kazakhstan's ODA system was the development and implementation of pilot projects, which are expected to facilitate further maturation and improvement of the country's ODA mechanisms. By 2019, the government of Kazakhstan implemented several pilot ODA projects: the pilot project of Kazakhstan's ODA for partner countries in Central Asia designed in close cooperation with the UNDP Mission in Kazakhstan and the Israeli Agency for International Cooperation "MASHAV" (2017), and the project titled "Assistance to Kazakhstan in cooperation with Afghanistan in the field of official development assistance" (2017–2018) developed with the support of UNDP and the Ministry of Foreign Affairs of Japan.[20]

Former Foreign Minister Erlan Idrissov, who was the first person to introduce the idea of establishing Kazakhstan as an official development aid donor, emphasized in an interview with the author that Kazakhstan was the first donor in Eurasia to pass relevant laws on national system of official development assistance with the help of the UNDP and the OECD—something other regional contributors (Russia and Azerbaijan) were lacking at the time. He maintained that Kazakhstan could be called a "pioneer" when it comes to the adoption of such legislation, which at the time had no analogues in the CIS space. In order to implement the Law of the Republic of Kazakhstan "On Official Development Assistance", the Ministry of Foreign Affairs adopted a number of by-laws and regulations, such as Orders of the Minister of Foreign Affairs of the Republic of Kazakhstan "On Approval of the Rules for Interaction between Government Bodies and Organizations in the Field of ODA" of February 6, 2015, and "On Approval of the Form of a Project Proposal of ODA" of February 6, 2015 (Graph 4.1).[21]

It should be noted that on January 31, 2017, a Decree of the President of the Republic of Kazakhstan "On approving the main directions of state policy in the field of ODA for 2017–2020" (hereinafter referred to as ONGP) was adopted in accordance with Article 6 of Kazakhstan's Law on Official Development Assistance. The ONGPs for 2017–2020 are medium term in nature and are aligned with Kazakhstan's foreign policy priorities. They are also synchronized with the Concept of the

Graph 4.1 Amount of Kazakh aid provided (*Source* MFA [Interview 4, 2018])

Foreign Policy of the Republic of Kazakhstan for the period up to 2020. The document is primarily aimed at determining geographic and sectoral priorities for the country's ODA activities, as well as the forms and mechanisms of financing, and key parameters and instruments of engagement. The government is currently developing a draft ONGP for the next five-year period 2021–2025.[22]

Idrissov added that the project is, "first and foremost, directed at the systematization of the already existing Kazakhstan's official foreign aid provided to other countries, since the presence of the national ODA system is one of the attributes of a developed state".[23] Similarly, former First Deputy Minister of Foreign Affairs of Kazakhstan Rapil Zhoshybayev in his interview with Astana Times stressed the fact that the country had already been a significant aid donor in the region having allocated US$100 million over the past 10 years before the adoption of the appropriate laws.

He also explained that the KazAID initiative ought to systemize Kazakhstan's development assistance contributions and does not imply an increase in the country's aid provision levels per se.[24] During his speech at the VIII Astana Economic Forum "Africa – the World's Next Economic Driver", Erlan Idrissov (2015) mentioned that the main focus of KazAID is twofold: provision of financial assistance and knowledge transfer. Foreign Minister pointed out that the event has a historical significance for the country symbolizing its transition to the next development stage (ibid.). Although at the time the government was yet to finalize the establishment of the official agency for the provision of international development assistance—KazAID—the state enjoyed the support of various international development assistance institutions.

During his speech at the Government Hour, Maulen Ashimbayev, the former Chairman of the Committee for International Affairs, Defense and Security of the Mazhilis of Parliament of Kazakhstan, too, stressed Kazakhstan's role as the first country in the Commonwealth of Independent States (CIS) to adopt the Law on Official Development Assistance back in 2014.[25] Having discussed his opinion on the main reasons of the country's continuous foreign aid work, Ashimbayev stated:

> "I think that (politics of isolationism and national protectionism) is a futile path. Especially considering the fact that no state can prosper in the long-term when its neighboring countries are experiencing serious challenges and hardships".

The initiative was also backed up by then Vice-Chairperson of the Mazhilis Bozhko, who in an interview with PervyiKanal Kazakhstan (2016) emphasized that aid, provided by the country, has helped to attract investors. According to Bozhko, US$250 billion has been invested into the Kazakhstani economy since the state's independence.

As seen in Graph 4.2, the amount of aid provided by the Kazakhstani government in 2014 was 293% larger than the previous year's level. In fact, the state continued to expand its Net ODA by making a contribution of approximately $43 million in 2015 (about 29% increase from the 2014 level). Interestingly, as mentioned above, such increase in aid spending coincides with a sharp GDP decline, which the country experienced in 2013.[26]

The main recipient of Kazakh aid, since its official launch, has been Afghanistan, contributions to which significantly outweigh Kazakhstan's donations to other neighboring countries (Graph 4.2).

Over the last few years, the state's ODA allocation patterns have been subject to some changes, but the main trends remained the same. For example, Tajikistan received US$7.1 million in development assistance from Kazakhstan in 2015—5.5 million more than the previous year (US$1.6 million).

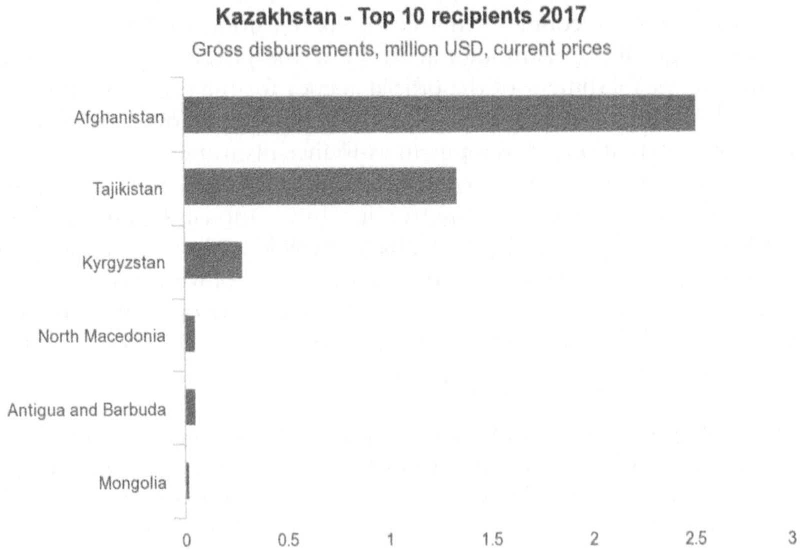

Graph 4.2 Top recipients—Kazakhstan ODA (2017) (*Source* OECD [2019])[27]

Moreover, Kazakhstan's contribution to Ukraine has risen threefold in 2015 (US$1.27 million) compared to 2014 levels (US$0.38 million). The reverse trend can be observed in regard to Kyrgyzstan, which was allocated only US$0.36 million in 2015 as opposed to US$6.5 million in 2014. Kazakhstan's contribution to Afghanistan, the country's main aid recipient, has also decreased (from US$12.8 million to US$9.13 million), although remaining relatively high.

According to the official data provided to the author by the Ministry of Foreign Affairs of the Republic of Kazakhstan, since its independence Kazakhstan has distributed approximately 542 million US dollars in the form of foreign assistance to its neighbors in Central Asia and beyond. This amounts to about 0.024% of the country's total GDP for the period from 1996 to 2018 according to the Committee on Statistics of the Ministry of National Economy of the Republic of Kazakhstan.[28]

Key Features and Characteristics of Kazakh Aid

As it has been revealed through the conducted interviews with Kazakh ODA officials, the structure of Kazakh aid remains in a state of continuous development. Currently, Kazakhstan's foreign aid architecture is confined within the Ministry of Foreign Affairs of the Republic of Kazakhstan.[29] The responsible MFA body that was designed to oversees the conducted work is Foreign Economic Policy Department, which includes the Official Development Assistance Administration.[30]

The study also reveals several core-guiding principles of Kazakh foreign aid.

First, horizontal models of cooperation, as well as mutual solidarity and equality lie at the heart of how Kazakhstan understands development aid provision. Although it has not been clearly stated in the Concept on ODA, it becomes evident from the analysis that Kazakhstan sees itself as a part of the South-South Cooperation (SSC)—a broad cooperation framework that distinguishes from the North–South Cooperation (NSC) due to its emphasis on the notion of horizontality.

To be more specific, SSC providers declare that their engagement with recipients is horizontal—which means it is based on mutual solidarity and should be seen as cooperation between equal partners that ought to benefit all parties involved.[31] The language Kazakhstani officials choose when referring to the national aid strategy is of particular interest. Recipient countries are referred to as "partners", which once again stresses the horizontal power distribution under Kazakhstan's ODA. This goes in line with the widespread practice among the "emerging" donor countries that exhibit reluctance to call themselves "donors" and instead, prefer to be called "development partners". On top of that, they often do not depict their assistance as delivery of "aid" per se, but rather portray it as a process of building "development partnerships" based on solidarity and mutual respect (Fig. 4.2).

According to Kazakh governmental officials in the field of ODA, "the terminology is extremely important. We work closely with representatives of other countries, and our partners sometimes have a mixed reaction to the choices we make in regard to the terms with which we appeal to others. For example, our partners prefer to be called "partners", rather than "recipient countries". We respect their opinion. We pay quite serious attention to this, and we try to take into account if our partners in general

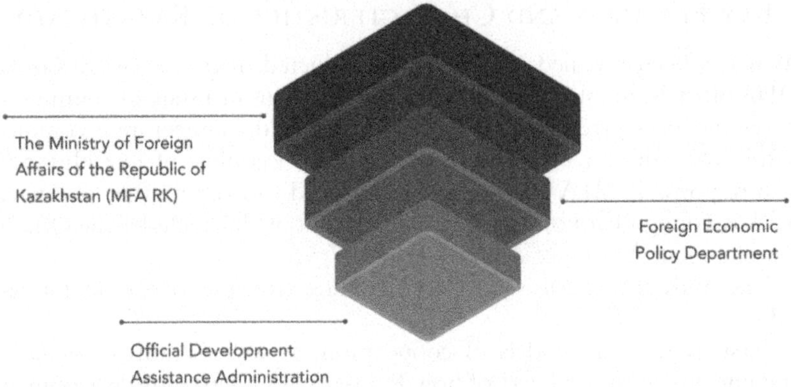

Fig. 4.2 Kazakh ODA institutional structure (Author's compilation based on fieldwork)

have a desire to cooperate, and if they are interested in us assisting their development".[32]

Second, the principle of non-interference is at the core of Kazakhstan's development aid-giving. It has been clearly stated that the country would not intervene into recipients' domestic affairs and governmental processes due to the fact that Kazakhstan upholds equality and mutually beneficial partnership, and "interacts with aid recipient-countries on an equal footing".[33]

The next guiding principle of Kazakhstan's ODA distribution model is the principle of no political conditionality. Kazakhstan benefits from political neutrality and does not seek to use aid as a tool to promote any ideological interests; thus, there is no explicitly articulated conditionality in terms of human rights and democratic practices associated with Kazakh aid. Kazakhstan does not generally call for institutional change: adherence to liberal democratic principles and neoliberalism, as well as fostering civil rights, good governance and human rights abroad are not on the Kazakh agenda.

In addition, prioritizing technical cooperation for capacity development has been emphasized by the local policymakers to be one of the main features of Kazakh aid. Kazakhstan highlights that the main purpose of its aid is to assist partner countries in building their self-development capacity, while the state's aid strategy rests on principles of respect for state sovereignty and national interests of their partners. The priority is given to technical cooperation[34] that is seen as the main approach to recipients' capacity development, which is enabled through knowledge, skills and technology transfer in the areas that Kazakhstan has a comparative advantage in. This is perceived to be a crucial instrument in assisting partner countries in the process of building their capability for leading and managing their own development aimed at stimulating economic growth and reducing poverty.

Finally, focused assistance is the final core-guiding principle of Kazakh aid provision. Kazakhstan identified the following sectors as priority areas for cooperation: education; health; agriculture and food security; environment protection; conflict management and security; combating transnational crime; public policy management.

As the above-provided discussion elucidates, Kazakhstan has discursively constructed itself as a "development cooperation partner", adopting the discourse of mutual benefit, respect for sovereignty and non-interference and associating oneself with "emerging donors" community. At the same time, however, it also selectively complies with policies and practices advocated by "traditional donors" (focused assistance, donor harmonization and attention to social development among others), which will be discussed in detail in the following sections.

During one of the conducted interviews with Kazakh ODA governmental officials, Kazakhstan's approach to Official Development Assistance was summarized as follows:

> We pay a lot of attention to the cooperation with the OECD. Our priority is joining the OECD and pulling our development to the level of the OECD. The approaches adopted by the Development Assistance Committee are the gold standard, which we cannot ignore. The world experience is concentrated there, and we want to be a member of this club (meaning OECD).
>
> But if we focus on the DAC standards, this does not mean that we cannot experiment, and take a closer look at South-South cooperation.
>
> As a systemic donor, we take the first steps, we probe the soil, we observe. Time will pass, and we will regard ourselves as a solid donor. It is possible we will be like traditional donors, non-traditional donors or even a hybrid. Most likely it will be a hybrid. We are trying to find the best approach. Even when it comes to legislation, we try to be diplomats.[35]

To briefly summarize the analysis thus far, it has been demonstrated that Kazakhstan embraces a hybrid identity as a foreign aid donor. In other words, the combination of features and characteristics pertaining to both emerging and traditional donors resulted in the construction of the distinct patterns of Kazakh development aid policy. Since a donor's identity is not pre-given, it is important to examine what factors account for the construction of these particular aid patterns of Kazakh donorship and how the created aid modality can be explained. In line with this, the second half of this book examines both domestic and international factors that condition Kazakhstan's donor identity and, subsequently, its interests.

The Domestic Context and Interests of Stakeholders: The Drafting of the Law on ODA

In April 2013, Kazakhstan presented the ODA Concept of the Republic of Kazakhstan—the document ought to set the roadmap of the state's development aid initiative. The Kazakh national system of ODA was established under the Ministry of Foreign Affairs (MFA) of Kazakhstan with the operating budget of 0.01% of GDP for the purpose of providing development assistance primarily to the countries in its immediate neighborhood.

The Law of the Republic of Kazakhstan "On Official Development Assistance" has been drafted through a collaborative process involving different bodies. For example, members of the Ak Zhol Democratic Party[36] (2014) made a series of proposals to the project. The Party's suggestions to include "reduction of unemployment" to the list of the main goals and objectives and "fight against corruption" to the list of sectoral priorities were declined. It could be explained by Kazakhstan's reluctance to interfere in others' internal affairs, which addressing such issues as eradication of unemployment and corruption sometimes require, since both problems are usually approached through the promotion of institutional change. Moreover, Kazakhstan has often been described by international experts as a state that has been struggling with a high level of internal corruption itself. Transparency International (2016) put Kazakhstan in the list of top 50 most corrupt countries in the world; therefore, some could argue that Kazakhstan may not be the perfect fit for advising its partners on how to eliminate or reduce domestic corruption. In contrast, other two suggestions (inclusion of "improvement of business climate" and "land use and natural resource management" to the list of sectoral priorities of the national aid) have received favorable consideration and eventually appeared in the Official Law on ODA. Both of these revolve around economic development, not political transformations,[37] which could explain why the government eventually approved these less politically sensitive proposals.

In an interview, the head of the Kazakh ODA department explained that:

> The law itself has changed a lot, from its very first draft version to the latest one. The decision did not go down from above. Most of the changes were made when the draft of the law passed through both the Lower and Upper House of Parliament. Several proposals were made by parliamentarians. There was a constructive dialogue. For example, the law does not indicate the entire list of priority sectors, and we did it on purpose to give ourselves some flexibility. In the section on the priority sectors in the law, there is a "loophole" for us called "and other sectors".[38]

These were not the only changes introduced to the Law, however. As such, the Senate—the Upper House of the Parliament—suggested amendments ought to clarify the powers invested in the government in accordance with the constitutional law of the Republic of Kazakhstan "On the Government of the Republic of Kazakhstan".[39] The *Mazhilis* (2014) approved the introduced modification, which did not change the conceptual framework of the initiative.

Having analyzed the differences between the two versions, it can be concluded that the authority of the government over the national aid agency has eventually been expanded with the body not only being responsible for the establishment of KazAID, but also having the legal capacity to reorganize and/or shut it down. Nevertheless, the Senate has also proposed to limit the role the government played in the sphere of ODA. For instance, the original draft of the Law equipped the government with the power to "approve policy documents in the field of official development assistance", but the updated version of the document stated that the Government of the Republic of Kazakhstan was to "develop the main directions of the state policy of the Republic of Kazakhstan in the sphere of ODA and submit them for approval to the President of the Republic of Kazakhstan".

> There were also heated discussions in the Senate. This bill is one of a kind in the history of Kazakhstan, so it aroused a lot of interest in the Parliament. I personally defended this bill at the Parliament meeting. I believe that this is normal, since the President determines the country's foreign policy, and ODA is connected with Kazakhstan's foreign policy for 2014-2020.
>
> But naturally, the important role of the Parliament and the government remains. Budget funds are allocated from the national budget. I also want to add that if the bill successfully passed through the Parliament, then it means that all those participating in the discussion are satisfied with the version that has been adopted. This means that everyone has come to a consensus.[40]

In other words, the President has the ultimate authority over Kazakhstani ODA activities. Such power dynamics within Kazakhstan's aid program mirrors the political power structure within the country with the most power invested in the President.

Notes

1. De Cordier, B. (2014). Kazakhstan and Azerbaijan as donors of humanitarian aid: Has the diversification of aid channels and donors reached southern eurasia? *Central Asia and the Caucasus, 15*(4).
2. Kazakhstan provided KZT 10 bln humanitarian aid to foreign nations. (2017, March 13). *Kazinform.*
3. As many as 91 non-DAC donors provided humanitarian relief in 2005.
4. Kazakhstan peredal gumanitarnuyu pomosh Syrii. (2017, January 6). *Tengrinews.kz.*
5. Kazakhstan discusses further aid to Syria with Russia, Red Cross, UN. (2016, October 11). *Sputnik.*
6. Kazakhstan provides humanitarian aid to Syria. (2017, January 6). *Ministry of Foreign Affairs of Republic of Kazakhstan.*
7. Seisembayeva (2017).
8. OCHA Annual Report 2015. (2016). United Nations Office for Coordination of Humanitarian Affairs.

9. Kazakhstan. (n.d.). United Nations for the Coordination of Humanitarian Affairs—Regional Office for the Caucasus and Central Asia.
10. Kazakhstan provided Afghanistan with funds to reconstruct the road Talukan-Kunduz-Shirhan-Bandar (see Nazarbayev, N. [2013, April 26]. *President Nazarbayev's Speech at the Almaty Ministerial Conference of the Istanbul Process on Afghanistan*).
11. Regional Development Cooperation Strategy (2014).
12. Nazarbayev, N. (2010, November 2). Nursultan Nazarbayev: V nashei druzhbe net nikakih sekretov with Vasilyev, A./ Interviewer. *Rossiyskaya Gazeta*.
13. Kazakhstan nameren aktivizitovat rabotu v kachestve strany – donora v ramkah Aziatskogo banka razvitiya (2014, April 22).
14. Kazakhstan hochet izbavitsya ot statusa poluchatelya bezvozmezdnoi pomoshi ADB. (2013, October 24). *Tengrinews*.
15. Interviewee 2, 2018.
16. Interviewee 1, 2017.
17. Interviewee 2, 2018.
18. Interview 1, 2017; Interview 4, 2018.
19. Interview 4, 2018.
20. Interview 5, 2018; Interview 6, 2019.
21. Interview 5, 2018.
22. Baigarin, M. (2014, October 29). Mazhilis odobril proekt, sistematiziruyushy pomosh razvitiyu drugih stran. *Kazinform*.
23. KazAid is key to Kazakh regional development, says Deputy FM. (2014, October 10). *Ministry of Foreign Affairs of the Republic of Kazakhstan*.
24. It is important that members of the Mazhilis of Parliament of Kazakhstan took an active participation in drafting the Law on Official Development Assistance, according to the source.
25. World Bank (2019).
26. OECD. (2019). Kazakhstan. In *Development co-operation profiles*. OECD Publishing.
27. Interview 5, 2018.
28. The diagram was prepared by the author.
29. Interview 4, 2018.
30. Concept of the Republic of Kazakhstan in the sphere of official development assistance. (2013). *Government of the Republic of Kazakhstan*.

31. Interview with the representative of the Ministry of Foreign Affairs, Foreign Economic Policy Department, Nur-Sultan, 2019 Interview 6, 2019.
32. Concept of the Republic of Kazakhstan in the sphere of official development assistance. (2013). *Government of the Republic of Kazakhstan*.
33. Ibid.
34. Interview 6, 2019.
35. Ak Zhol Democratic Party represents an opposition to the ruling political party in Kazakhstan—Nur Otan. As of the 2016 elections, Ak Zhol is the second most represented party in the Lower Chamber of Kazakhstan's Government—the Mazhilis.
36. Nazarbayev, N. (2011, January 28). *Address of the President of the Republic of Kazakhstan, Nursultan Nazarbayev, to the People of Kazakhstan*.
37. Interview 5, 2018.
38. Senat vernul v Mazhilis zakonoproekt ob oficialnoy pomoshi razvitiyu. (2014, November 20). *Today.kz*.
39. Interview 4, 2018.
40. Although the country has announced its preparedness to give lawmakers more power, it is still unclear how Kazakhstan's aid program is to be affected by these changes.

CHAPTER 5

New Actors Through Old Lenses?

Abstract This chapter focuses on Kazakhstan's pre-independence history and takes a closer look at the peculiarities of the Soviet modernization project. This chapter is based on the primary sources uncovered by the author in the archives in Kazakhstan and highlights the development programs implemented on the territory of modern-day Kazakhstan by the Soviet regime. This chapter examines whether certain aspects of Kazakhstan's history have affected its subsequent foreign aid policy choices, and if so, then how. Specifically, the Soviet emphasis on education and female emancipation will be discussed as the primary sources of influence for Kazakhstan's current development efforts abroad. The work shows that the Soviet legacy represents a crucial element, which has affected Kazakhstan's conceptualization and understanding of development. In other words, this chapter will analyze Kazakhstan's development aid projects in Central Asia and Afghanistan and will provide an explanation for how these programs have been influenced by Kazakhstan's identity as a former Soviet republic, aid recipient and ODA provider.

Keywords USSR · Soviet modernization · Third-Worldization · Education · Women emancipation · ODA projects

N. Insebayeva, *Modernity, Development and Decolonization of Knowledge in Central Asia*, Politics and History in Central Asia,
https://doi.org/10.1007/978-981-16-5117-5_5

So, why has Kazakhstan chosen to formulate and construct its aid modality the way we observe it today? As it was discussed in the previous chapter, the interests and voices of stakeholders that participated in the development of Kazakhstan's ODA scheme were taken into consideration and resulted in the modality described above.

Apart from that, however, this book argues that a combination of the Soviet legacy, Kazakhstan's experience as a recipient of Western foreign aid in the aftermath of the Soviet Union's collapse and international factors played a significant role in shaping Kazakhstan' foreign aid policy. To show this, this chapter is designed to briefly introduce the reader to the history of Kazakhstan as a subject of Soviet modernization project. In particular, by utilizing rare primary sources uncovered by the author in the archives during field trips to Kazakhstan. This section will give an overview of the Soviet policies pertaining to the development of the region and explain how Kazakhstan's experience as a former socialist republic has shaped its identity as a development aid provider.

Writing the history of Kazakhstan prior to the declaration of its independence and the dissolution of the Soviet Union has been a challenging task. Although not exclusive in this regard, the history of post-Soviet republics continues to be a battleground of competing, alternative narratives and new facts, which are constantly re-written and re-interpreted.

Regardless, the two main characteristics of Kazakhstan's past development—isolation from external influences and strong dependency on the Soviet "center"—make Kazakhstan an interesting case study, which distinguishes it from the traditional profile of foreign aid recipients, which later became foreign aid donors.

In addition, what makes Kazakhstan's case stand out further, at least from the perspective of development studies, is the country's "third-worldization" in the aftermath of the disintegration of the USSR. As explained by Estes and Somach (2006), for example, the fall of communism and the end of the Cold War transformed Kazakhstan (as well as other post-soviet states) from a member-state of one of the world's superpowers to an independent nation in transition. Although the concepts of the "First", "Second" and "Third World" have for a long time been recognized as outdated, in the early 1990s the term "Third World country" was widely used to refer to what experts now call "developing states". This practice can be explained by the fact that "the development discourse inevitably contained a geopolitical imagination that has shaped the meaning of development".[1] Such expressions as "First and

Third World, North and South, center and periphery" (ibid.) exemplify the point. Generally speaking, being labeled a Third World country meant being associated with and described as "backward", "stagnant", and "underdeveloped". While many specialists at the time resorted to this Cold War terminology when referring to some post-socialist states, in hindsight, it is difficult to categorize these nations as "underdeveloped", given their relatively high performance in certain areas. More specifically, the tight Soviet control and modernization initiatives, implemented during the period of socialist rule, left a unique legacy in the form of high literacy rates, as well as significant impact of the Soviet-style female emancipation practices.

In other words, the peculiar history of post-Soviet nations, such as Kazakhstan, made it difficult to place them within the First-Third World geopolitical categories. In fact, arguments could be raised that Kazakhstan, which is located between Europe and Asia, at that time possessed the attributes of both of those classifications but did not quite fit into either of them. On the one hand, foreign actors had only interacted with Kazakhstan as a part of the Soviet Union—the superpower, which the West deemed strong enough to consider a threat. On the other hand, some may argue that the center-periphery structure of the USSR and inequality among the socialist republics suggest that Kazakhstan could be seen as a third-world country within a more developed state.

It must be noted, however, that Kazakh SSR played an important part in the Soviet centralized, non-market, planned economy. More specifically, while lacking in industrialization and depending on the "center" in other spheres[2] (e.g., infrastructure development, government subsidies), Kazakhstan was one of the major Soviet producers of raw materials.[3] As there was a high level of interdependence among the Soviet socialist republics and no access to outside partners, the members of the USSR relied on each other as essential elements of their supply chain. For example, in the Central Asian case, international trade constituted as little as 10–15% of their total trade. Apart from that, the vast Kazakh territory was also utilized by the Soviet regime as a nuclear testing site and the base of operations for the Soviet space program. The government also built important infrastructure (e.g., roads, hospitals, schools, etc.), which helped to improve the quality of life in Kazakh SSR. Therefore, this provides an insight into the level of Kazakhstan's dependency on the system of planning and distribution set out by Moscow, and sheds light on the overwhelming impact of the fall of the Soviet Union on the country's socioeconomic situation.

After several years since the collapse of the communist regime in Kazakhstan, many experts have started to point at the parallels between Moscow's relations with the peripheral areas of the Soviet Union, including Kazakhstan, and the colonial power structures involving "first world" colonizers and their "Third World" subjects. Despite these views on the Soviet rule, there were substantial differences between the communist expansion model and colonialism in its traditional sense. Specifically, while European colonial agenda was founded upon the capitalist aspirations, the goal of the USSR was to establish an integral communist space based on socialist ideology. As Luong (2004, p. 21) puts it, even though the Soviet ideals were aggressively implanted in Kazakhstan, over time they have grown "strong indigenous roots there".

As it has been previously mentioned, another crucial component of Kazakhstan's profile, which set it aside from traditional recipients of development aid at the time, was its experience as a subject of the Soviet modernization project. In other words, what distinguished Kazakhstan from former colonies and "Third World" countries was that despite initial economic struggles, the state could boast high levels of literacy, education and professional training among its population, as well as possession of certain technology and infrastructure.[4] While, to nobody's surprise, Kazakhstan was outperformed by bigger post-Soviet economies, such as the Baltic states, it still had the features of both developing and developed nations and had higher levels of human development than its Southern neighbors.[5]

Therefore, the positive outcomes of the Soviet modernization policy placed Kazakhstan ahead of many other foreign aid recipients. For instance, Ruth Mandel (1998, p. 632) argued that on many scales, except the devastating economic legacy of central planning, the post-socialist republics could be considered "highly developed". Mandel also points out that due to this, donors' knowledge and experience from interacting with the "Third World" aid recipients have little relevance in the case of the former Soviet states. In other words, the results of Kazakhstan's development during its membership in the USSR in many regards have elevated its position relative to the traditional understanding of the Third World countries. Hence, the discussed features of Kazakhstan's case further point at the arbitrary nature of this categorization and related assumptions.

It is, thus, interesting to uncover how the unique case of Kazakhstan's development can influence our current understanding of and knowledge about foreign aid, development discourses and practices. The following section will examine two cases and prominent achievements of the Soviet modernization project in Kazakhstan, which relate to the rest of this book: education and emancipation of women.

The Soviet Modernization Project: Education

One of the prominent achievements of the Soviet modernization project was a series of educational reforms. Specifically, the USSR strategy has produced some positive outcomes through extending elementary and secondary education to non-Russian nationalities on a more equal basis, and through promoting large-scale education in the minority (non-Russian) languages. For example, the Soviet policy of "nativization" or "korenizatsiya", which was introduced in the early 1920s and enforced until early 1930s, is often cited as one of the most important aspects of the Soviet regime's efforts in eradication of illiteracy and promotion of universal compulsory education.

The project aimed at the elimination of illiteracy in Kirgiz Autonomous Soviet Socialist Republic (later renamed to Kazakh Soviet Socialist Republic—Kazakh SSR[6]) was put forward in 1920. This was a rather challenging endeavor, given that one of the many legacies of the Tsarist rule was an overwhelmingly low level of education in the Kazakh Steppe—95% of the population were illiterate.[7] Despite the fact that in the early 1920s, the total of 89,000 people completed literacy training, the archival documents of that time suggest that the Kazakh population was barely affected by the introduced policies.[8] To be more specific, the liquidation of illiteracy during that period has mainly affected the Red Army units, workers and partly the peasantry.[9]

This trend began to change in 1923–1924. During this year, there were 611 seasonal teaching facilities in operation, of which 155 were Kirgiz (Kazakh).[10] Approximately 16,000 illiterate citizens completed courses, and Kirgiz students constituted about 24% of all trained (or 3,824 people). 82% of these 16,000 were representatives of the aul[11] and rural population, and the remaining 18% were members of various professional organizations. Thus, by the beginning of 1925, after five years from the start of formal organized literacy efforts, the Soviet regime was able to train as many as 105,000 people.

According to the statistics presented by the Kazakh Regional Committee of the Communist Party, in 1925, the total number of illiterates in the Kazakh SSR between the ages of 14 and 40 was equal to 1,200,000 people, of which 800,000 were Kazakh. By the end of the five-year period, i.e., by 1932, Glavpolitprosvet[12] planned to reach an ambitious target of educating 947,580 people, which at the time constituted 46% of the total number of illiterates.

Teaching in Kirgiz schools of the first degree—"shkoly pervoi stupeni" (primary schools)—was conducted in the native language—Kazakh. The Russian language was introduced to the curriculum starting from the third year of study, as a separate subject. However, due to the fact that most schools of that type only offered three-year (and sometimes two-year) training, on top of the fact that few Kazakh instructors were fluent in Russian, in reality the Russian language classes were not offered in the majority of these schools at the time.

The analysis of these archival documents points that there were rare instances when the public requested teaching in Kazakh schools (kirshkoly) be conducted in Russian rather than in their mother tongue. This phenomenon was explained to have been caused by two primary factors. First, this was due to the fact that Russian language proficiency presented many opportunities and served as a gateway to various special educational institutions. Second, such public demands were said to be partially influenced by the population's unfavorable perception of Kazakh teachers, whose qualifications were believed to be lower than those of Russian educators.

Despite these rare exceptions, however, the reports uncovered during fieldwork suggest that, overall, the Kirgizization (Kazakhization) of schools of the first degree was implemented almost completely. This also applied to orphanages, where teaching was conducted in the native language, although the number of Kazakh orphanages at the time equaled 15—a relatively small amount compared to a total of 167 Russian orphanages.

The language situation was not as promising in vocational educational institutions, where the process of Kirgizization was substantially slower. Of all educational institutions of "Profobr" (professional education), only pedagogical schools trained students in their mother tongue. In other "Profobr" colleges, Kazakh language was incorporated into the curriculum as a mandatory subject. Moreover, the Soviet regime believed that it was impossible to carry out teaching in Kazakh at the institutions of the second degree—"shkoly vtoroy stupeni" (middle schools)—due to the fact that there were no corresponding prerequisites for this. Such prerequisites were: (a) the development of a cadre of fully qualified professionals for this type of schools and (b) the publication of textbooks and educational literature in Kazakh language.

The archival materials dating back to the early 1920s shed light on the situation regarding training of the Kirgiz teacher workforce. More specifically, Kirgiz teacher training at the time was conducted at five educational institutions—Kirgiz Institute of Public Education and four Pedagogical Colleges (Pedteknikum). As of 1925, there were a total of 769 Kirgiz students pursuing their education at Pedagogical Colleges, with 663 enrolled in Kirgiz institutions and 106 receiving training at Russian schools. During the time this report was published, there were no graduates from Kirgiz Pedagogical Colleges (Kirpedteknikums) due to the fact that these educational institutions were established only a couple of years prior. However, the materials stated that the first graduating class was expected to consist of up to 25 people (Graph 5.1).

It is documented that "the lack of Kirgiz teachers and their poor general education and political training" has already become an evident area of concern for the regime by the late 1922, which required a consolidated effort toward teacher retraining. Therefore, during the summer of 1923, 795 teachers, or 14% of the total school workforce, passed through government-organized short-term courses. Kirgiz educators constituted 12.7% of all participants (147 people), while the rest were Russian. The following year, these numbers have significantly increased with 1,300 Sotsvos (system of social education) workers completing the retraining courses, of which 587 students were Kirgiz (46%), 685 were Russian (52%) and 28 were people of other ethnicities (2%). What this data shows is that in a short period of time—within two years of the commencement of the program—as many as 38.5% of Sotsvos employees passed through the system (63.6% Kirgiz, 33.3% Russian, other 3%).

Although the positive outcomes of this scheme have been acknowledged, the overall assessment of the final results did not portray a particularly optimistic picture. It has been recognized that the retraining initiative has noticeably shifted teaching to be more aligned with the Soviet Party agenda and has given impetus to further self-development and learning. At the same time, the report states that, given the low general education level of Kirgiz teachers, they could not fully benefit from the retraining scheme. In other words, the quality of Kirgiz teachers

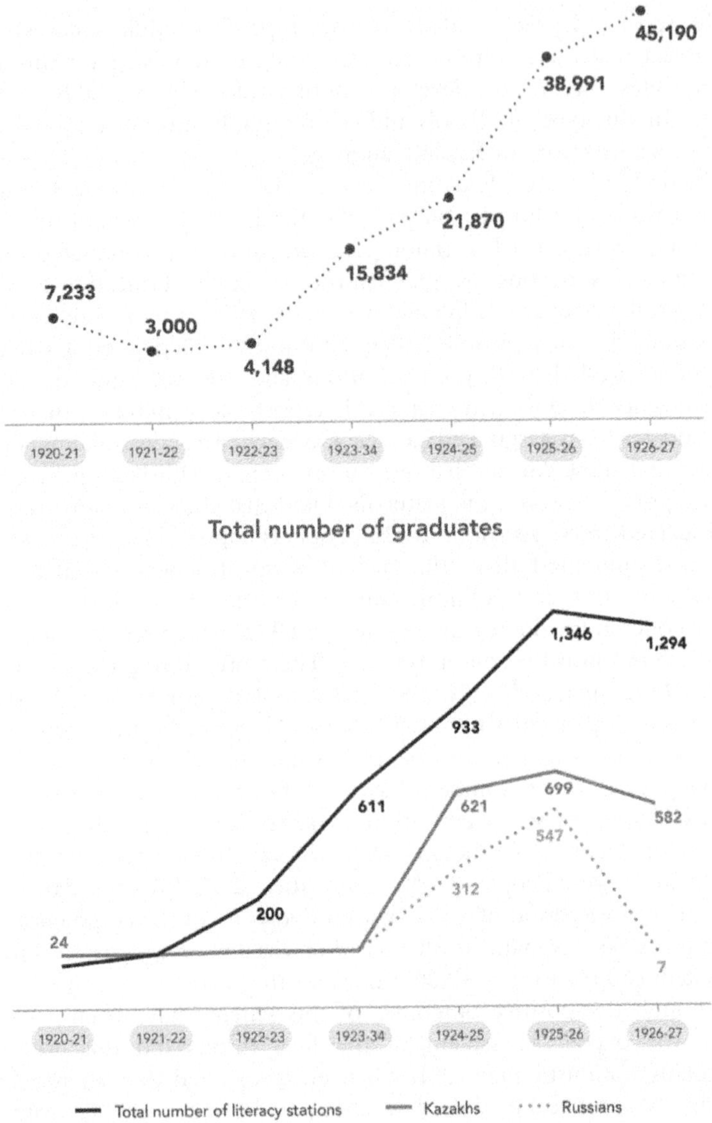

Graph 5.1 Statistics on the result of eradication of literacy in Kirgiz ASSR/Kazakh SSR

was believed to be so low that the introduction of short-term courses was not enough to address all existing knowledge gaps. A more solid effort was needed to tackle this challenge. It was also noted that the impact and significance of the offered retraining programs would increase if along with the courses Kirgiz teachers ("kiruchistel'stvo") had adequate pedagogical literature.[13]

Against this background, the Soviet administration at the time made the decision to establish teaching in most educational institutions of type two in Russian. This decision was justified on the basis of the lack of qualified Kirgiz teachers and lack of textbooks and teaching aids, which was considered to be the main cause why mother tongue-based programs in schools could not give promising results.

When it comes to institutions of higher education in the USSR, the dominant language of training was Russian, which many experts have since interpreted as national discrimination.[14] While the use of a uniform language in certain areas, such as technology and applied sciences, could be justified from the perspective of a more efficient intercultural communication and exchange, the relative lack of similar training offered in non-Russian languages limited access to education for the majority of Central Asian titular nations. For instance, DeWitt (1961) shows that in the late 1950s approximately 1000 students from Kirgiz SSR were forced to terminate their enrollment in universities due to their limited Russian language proficiency. This, in turn, led to the underrepresentation of indigenous population at workplaces during that period of time. Despite the controversy surrounding the favorable treatment of the Russian language, however, the overall literacy and education rates in Central Asia have continued to rise. In addition, it is important to note that the Soviet regime has also adopted a series of policies and measures that would promote participation of non-Russian students in higher education, which will be discussed further.

The Educational Legacy: Soviet Higher and Professional Education

An important component of the Soviet modernization project in Kirgiz ASSR (Kazakh SSR) was the establishment of first higher educational institutions[15] on the territory of what is now known as the Republic of Kazakhstan. Starting from the 1920s, the Soviet regime pursued an ambitious higher education agenda[16] for the purpose of expanding its educational system and preparing local experts during the period of "korenizatsiya".

This was also reflected in the professional hierarchy, where degrees in higher education were considered to be the gateway to virtually all respectable positions.[17] During this period, the number of Kazakhs in higher education across the USSR started to significantly grow. If according to the 1927 educational census, Kazakh students, who pursued higher education in different parts of the Soviet Union, constituted only 0.08% (133 people), the number has continuously risen as time progressed.[18] After several decades of state-enforced educational policies, Kazakh representation in higher education has grown closer to the nationality's share in the Soviet population. Nicholas DeWitt (1961),[19] for instance, identified that Soviet educational system pertaining to university admission during the 1950s incorporated nationality quotas, which were roughly proportional to the size of a group relative to the total USSR population. Indeed, data shows that Kazakhs were among the Soviet nations given a preferential quota, and as of 1959, the number of Kazakh students in higher education was equal to 69,900 (given that the population of Kazakh SSR was 3,622,000).[20]

Therefore, aside from ensuring wider enrollment of non-Russian students in the local institutions of higher education, some efforts have been directed at creating educational opportunities for non-Russians to study in other Soviet states. In an attempt to assist socialist republics in their path of developing local national "intelligentsia" (well-educated class), the regime has implemented a system of admission quotas, better known until 1930s as "sistema bronirovaniya mest" (placement reservation system).[21] The Ministry of Higher and Specialized Secondary Education allocated a set number of non-competitive admissions to prestigious universities in Moscow, Leningrad, Kazan, Sverdlovsk and other cities to the students from non-Russian republics. Historical documents suggest that in order to meet the quotas, university leadership would sometimes resort to granting these admissions to non-Russian students without secondary school diplomas,[22] with an expectation that those could fill the gaps in their knowledge during their studies.

On top of that, exchange programs catered to advanced students from non-Russian republics were a common practice and offered an opportunity for those excelling in their studies to complete their education at the institutions in central cities of the USSR. This initiative was primarily intended to cover the areas of study, in which non-Russian republics were not able to offer competitive high-level education. Upon graduating from those central universities, young specialists were sent back for assignment to the country they originally came from.

Figure 5.1 shows the number of students from Kazakh SSR on secondments in Russian universities in 1925 (primary data obtained by the author).[23]

Fig. 5.1 Kazakh SSR students on secondments in Russian universities in 1925 (Author's compilation. *Source* Archival materials)

To assist students in their pursuit of education, the Soviet regime has also designed the state scholarship policy, which targeted poor youth from the peasant-worker families. Special scholarship funds were allocated from the state budget to technical schools and courses. In the case of a limited number of state budget-funded scholarships, the local budget was used to cover for extra expenses. State universities were awarded national scholarships; however, due to their small size, the Council of People's Commissars of Kazakh SSR organized a special fund to grant additional benefits to the state-provided scholarships.[24] Generally, public education was funded through the state and local budgets, as well as the aforementioned special funds. The latter were collected through public contributions for the maintenance of colloquial schools, law school fees and farm income at educational institutions (Fig. 5.2).[25]

On top of establishing and actively facilitating higher education, an important achievement of Soviet educational reforms was the promotion of professional (special secondary) education among the population. As shown by the archival documents,[26] prior to the Bolshevik revolution, there was no organized system of professional education on the territory of modern Kazakhstan. At the time, the network of educational institutions was limited to around 50: 3 vocational schools in Semipalatinsk, Turgay and Uralsk; 4 agricultural schools in Almaty, Petropavlovsk, Semipalatinsk and Uralsk; up to 30 pedagogical classes at city schools and women's gymnasiums in regional and district cities; 3 teacher training courses in Aktyubinsk, Guryev and Kustanai; 8 teacher seminaries and teacher schools in Akmolinsk, Aktyubinsk, Almaty, Orenburg, Semipalatinsk, Uralsk and Ustkamenogorsk; and 1 teacher institute in Orenburg. However, as a result of the Soviet efforts, the number of professional educational institutions and qualified personnel has started to rapidly grow (Fig. 5.3).[27]

The Soviet Style Women Emancipation

Another interesting and important aspect of the Soviet socialist agenda, which is relevant to this research, was to achieve proclaimed equality between men and women. Although the nature of motivations behind this aspiration has been questioned by many, it is generally acknowledged that the regime accorded unprecedented attention to gender issues. This can be observed through a careful examination of the Soviet policies pertaining to women.

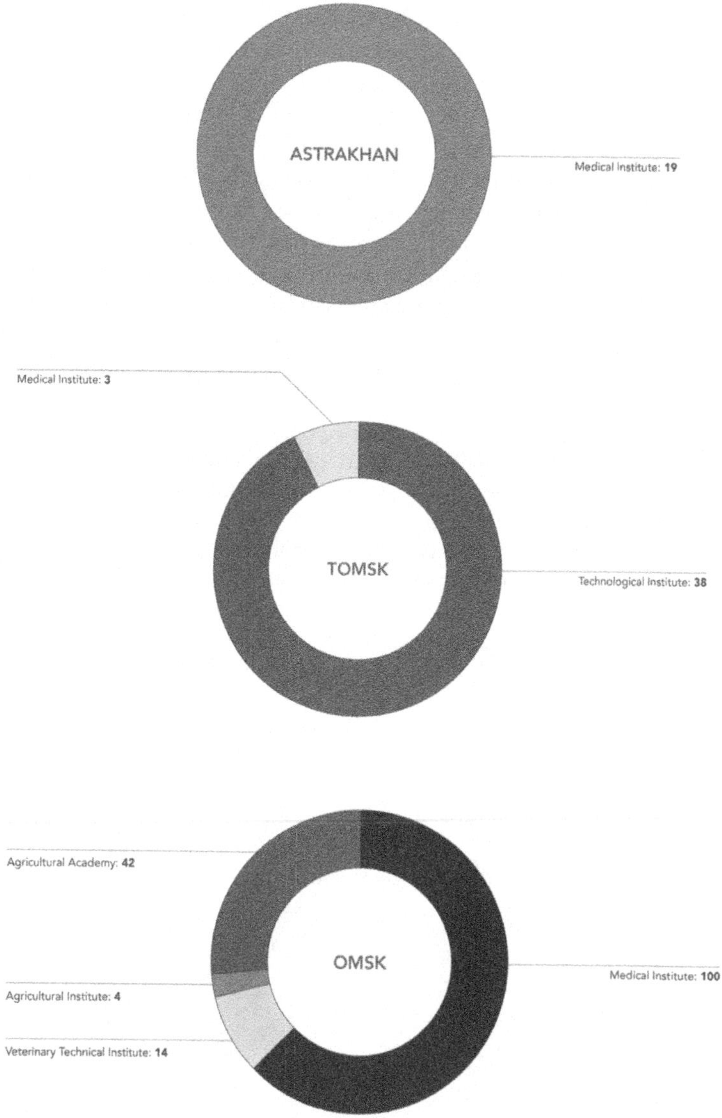

Fig. 5.2 Kazakh SSR students on secondments in Russian universities in 1925 (Author's compilation. *Source* Archival materials)

Even though the efficiency, consistency and targets of these efforts were sometimes questionable, the emancipation of women was without a doubt an integral part of the Soviet modernization project.[28]

The archival document titled "Report to the Women's Trainers Meeting" reiterates Lenin's and Stalin's rhetoric on the role of women by stating that the Communist Party has always considered tackling women's issues an objective of particular importance. The report quotes one of many Lenin's teachings, which proclaims that without ensuring women's participation in civil service, "there is nothing to be said not only about socialism, but also about complete and lasting democracy". It also features a part of the speech Stalin delivered at the 17th Congress of the All-Union Communist Party of Bolsheviks (VKPb), which goes as follows:

> "Women make up half of our country's population, they make up a huge army of labor, and their mission is to educate our children, our future generation, i.e. our future. That is why we cannot allow this vast army of working people to vegetate in darkness and ignorance. That is why we should also welcome the growing general activity of working women and their promotion to leadership positions, as an indisputable sign of the growth of our culture".[29]

Indeed, during the period of Soviet modernization, women were encouraged to take a more active role in the country's political life and in its

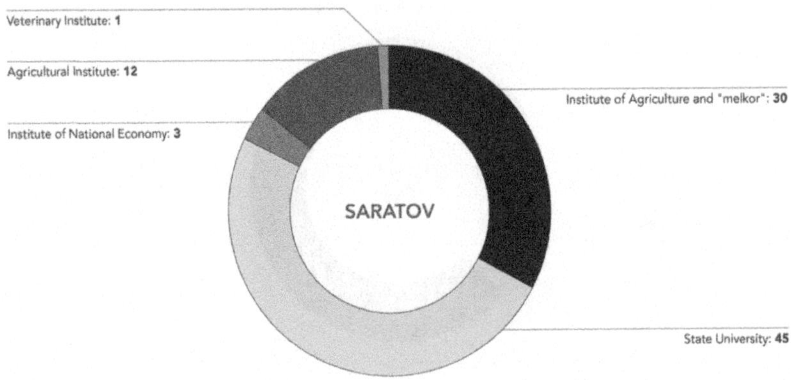

Fig. 5.3 Kazakh SSR students on secondments in Russian universities in 1925 (Author's compilation. *Source* Archival materials)

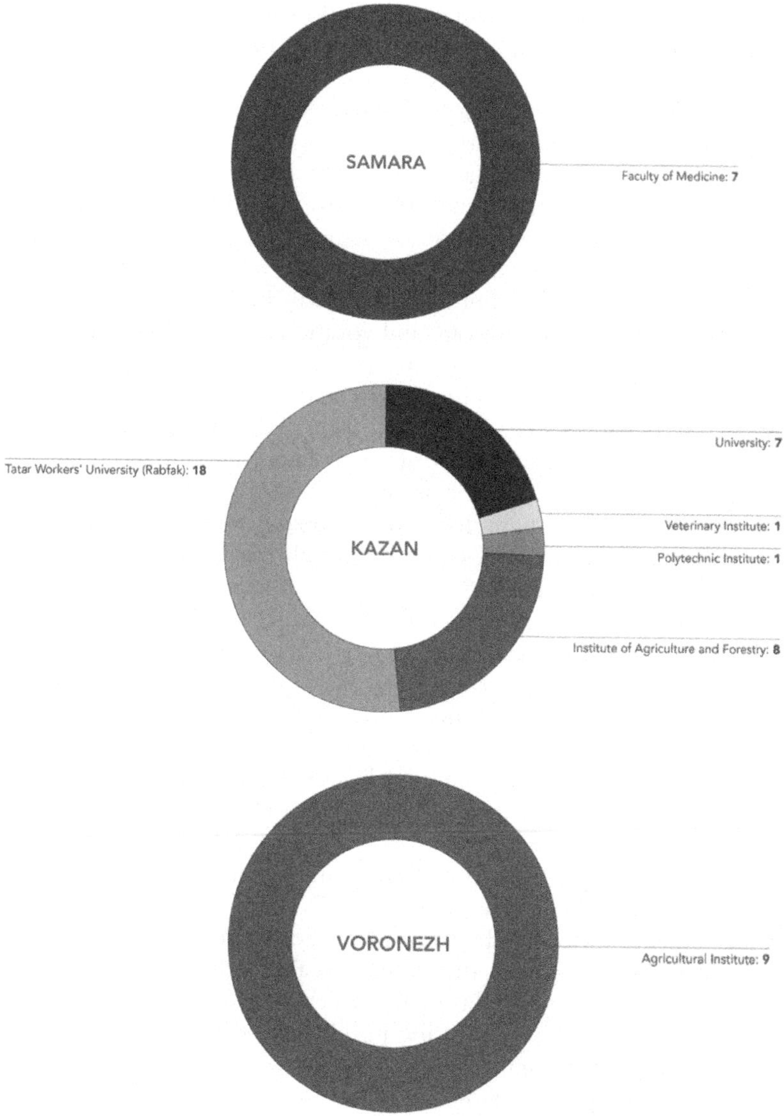

Fig. 5.3 (continued)

labor force. To assist the female population in this process, the Party granted women voting and property rights, instituted special educational quotas and provided some necessary social services. During this period of time, the Soviet regime[30] also prohibited the practices of polygamy and kalym (payment of bridewealth).[31]

The archival findings suggest that in the 1920s, activities concerning female empowerment in Kazakh SSR were carried out through general meetings, conferences, institutions of female delegates and the so-called red yurts. The latter was a campaign, which was adopted in the late 1920s to serve the nomadic and semi-nomadic female population and was aimed at promoting literacy, health care and vocational training among those.[32] In order to popularize the laws, which liberated women, and disseminate important knowledge on maternity and infant care, the "red yurts" initiative systematically organized discussion clubs or "kruzhki" centered on the laws on family and marriage, women's rights in the household, various diseases, as well as their prevention and treatment.[33]

Moreover, in their fight for gender equality, the Communist Party started offering institutional support through the Women's Department of the Central Committee Secretariat of All-Union Communist Party of Bolsheviks (Zhenotdel), in order to compensate for labor shortages and improve women's position in society. Zhenotdel was originally established in the early 1920s with an objective to improve the lives of Soviet, and in the Central Asian context—Muslim, women. Zhenotdels were not only preoccupied with encouraging wider female participation in the political, economic and cultural life of the country, but also advocated state-mandated maternity leaves and availability of public daycare institutions.[34]

Interestingly, the topic of maternity and infant care was one of the central focuses of the Soviet "female work", along with the promotion of women's contribution to the labor force. For instance, during fieldwork in the Kazakhstani archives, the author was able to find a document titled "Maternity and Infant Care Program for Female Delegates of Zhenotdel", which provides a rather interesting insight into the content of provided Soviet trainings in Kazakh SSR.[35]

The program goes as follows:

> The first part of the training was designed to last for 1 hour and focused on the topic of maternity and infant care and its significant role for the Soviet Union. The program emphasized that

maternity and infant care, before the revolution and at the time of program implementation, was one of the most important tasks for the Soviet rule. It was stated that the success and full implementation of the program would depend on the "growth of the culture- and economy-building" of the USSR.

In the second hour-long session, the delegates were educated on the social hygiene and its impact on maternity and infant health. More specifically, it was highlighted in the program that there is a causal relationship between population's economic conditions (from salary to housing conditions) and morbidity and mortality rates.

During the next 2-hour lecture, participants were taught about the main causes of child mortality in the first year of life. Four causes that have been listed are: gastrointestinal diseases, artificial and early feeding in the villages and auls, congenital weakness and poor heredity (syphilis, tuberculosis, alcohol), and infectious diseases.

The next topic covered in a 2-hour training was social causes of child mortality in the first year of life. Among those were: parents' social status, "illegitimate children", living conditions, social diseases and others.

Another 2-hour course focused on the fall in fertility by discussing the decline of fertility rates in different countries, and the reasons behind this phenomenon.

Next, perhaps one of the most ideologically charged parts of the training was a 2-hour-long session on the population's culture and its link to the birth rates. The topics covered included female labor and infertility, contraceptives and abortion (including the harms of abortion), and legislative protection of motherhood and infancy in the USSR. The most interesting discussion featured in this lecture was dedicated to the position of women and children in the capitalist states versus the Soviet Union, and it emphasized the impossibility of ensuring proper protection of maternity and infancy in the capitalist world.

The last two lectures, each 2 hour long, offered women information on relevant institutions and services (social and legal advice, nursery, etc.) designed to assist them in their everyday lives, and the role of Zhenotdels and their work in matters pertaining to maternity and infant care.

Some riveting parallels can be drawn between the programs implemented in Kazakh SSR, one of the Soviet Union republics at the time, and the development initiatives Kazakhstan is currently pursuing. The implications of this Soviet approach will be discussed in further detail. What must be noted, however, is the focus of the Soviet rule on the education component.

For instance, the archival records show that the 1928 plenum of the Communist Party raised some important issues related to women's education in Kazakh SSR. More specifically, the plenum emphasized the importance of taking "special measures to serve the needs of the female masses", called upon increasing female enrollment in secondary schools, and requested organizing "training groups specifically for women".[36] These efforts have soon started bringing positive results, and by the 1930s women of Kazakh SSR have slowly started to find employment outside their home. The number of working women has further risen during the World War II when increased pressures and labor shortages brought women into the workforce. As such, through its continuous efforts and economic and political circumstances, the Soviet rule was able to increase female labor force participation in Central Asia to up to 47%. On top of that, the regime managed to significantly lower female and infant mortality rate and significantly increase literacy rates among women and girls. Through these activities, the communist government aimed to build an image of a "Soviet woman", who is defined through her active role in the state's economy, culture and administration.[37]

In order to train and retrain Soviet female personnel, the Communist Party organized a series of courses in various regions of the country. In 1938, for example, there were 98 graduates from a 4-month program, and 400 women completed 10-day courses in the district and regional centers. Upon completing their training, "these comrades," as the document refers to them, were sent to do the Soviet work. As a part of this initiative, women were trained in stenography, typography, Soviet development and others. Unsurprisingly, one of the spheres that received particular Soviet attention, as mentioned above, was training of personnel for maternity and infancy care.[38]

Historical documents at the archives in Kazakhstan also cite one of the executive decisions related to female education announced at the 2nd Congress of the Communist (Bolshevik) Party of Kazakh SSR (CPbK), which took place in July 1938. In particular, the People's Commissariat of Agriculture was ordered to ensure that 30–40% of all students admitted to the courses of mass education were women. However, according to an assessment of Kazakh republican institutions and their work pertaining to women, conducted in 1940, this plan was not implemented, and women constituted only 5% of those under training. The documents suggest that the leaders of the land authorities and machine tractor stations (MTS) heavily underestimated the political significance of this issue. It was reported that the People's Commissariat of Agriculture (Narkomzem) and the People's Commissariat of State Farms (Narkomsovkhozov) did not make any efforts toward nominating women for managerial positions. Moreover, it was emphasized that there was not a single woman occupying a managerial role in the apparatus of Narkozem, Narkomsovkhozov, or in the regional district administrations of land bodies. In all of Kazakh SSR, only two women held the positions of directors for political matters at MTS.

The same report offers some interesting data on the structure of the People's Commissariat of Justice. More specifically, it is stated that after the 2nd Congress of CP(b)K, 12 women were nominated for managerial work, of which 9 were people's judges ("narsud'i") and 3 were members of regional courts. According to the source, 33 women were enrolled in the 2-year law school, which made up 25.7% of the total number of students. Moreover, 6 women were nominated through the Prosecutor's Office of the Kazakh SSR: 3 assistants to the regional prosecutor, 2 investigators and 1 district prosecutor.

The People's Commissariat of Health also received a positive evaluation, which explained that while no woman served as the head of any regional health department prior to the 2nd Congress, 2 people were nominated to take up the position shortly afterward, and 2 more women were nominated to join the apparatus of the People's Commissariat of Health as inspectors. The Commissariat has also organized training for approximately 20 people with the mission of educating workers on the topics of maternity and childcare. 300 females were studying in the republican obstetric school.

The presented findings point at an interesting feature of the Soviet approach to the "female" question. As seen from the documents and reports above, the Soviet regime has primarily shaped the view on women as workers and mothers, who depended on the state for their protection.[39] Despite the rhetoric based on the Soviet aspiration for equality between Soviet men and women, the regime has never questioned or contested the fundamental traditional gender roles, which guided the social, political and economic status of women in Kazakh SSR.

Despite this, however, the Zhenotdels soon ceased operation due to Stalin's order, which was the regime's way of declaring that the issues pertaining to gender equality in the Soviet Union have been solved. Not only did the work with women have for the most part stopped, but the position of women in the society was further reevaluated during World War II. Given the tremendous losses of human lives and resources, Stalinist regime emphasized the "natural" function of women as mothers and wives, and criminalized abortions with an intent to increase the birth rate. With the change of power in the Soviet Union, Khrushchev aimed to revert some of Stalin's policies and made certain attempts at addressing women's limited participation in the country's political life. Although abortions were re-legalized, the images of mothers remained an important part of the Soviet propaganda. This put pressure on women to fulfill their role as workers to compensate for declines in labor supply and economic productivity, and at the same time meet their duty of motherhood.[40] In fact, despite the changes in leadership and some variations in policies, this Soviet approach to female emancipation, which provided institutional support for women, but was not entirely "liberating", has persisted through the entire period of the Soviet rule.[41].

Even though Soviet-style female emancipation efforts established equality between genders in the face of the law and successfully facilitated an increase in female participation in the labor force, it barely affected the gender-related dynamics at home.[42] Hence, as stated above, this contradicting nature of the Soviet gender policy left Central Asian women trapped between the traditional roles they were ascribed by the regime and their culture, and the image of a Soviet working woman promoted by the government. Gal and Kligman (2000) also emphasize that although women were expected to contribute as much labor as men, they were not compensated equally. Moreover, as Posadskaya (1994) argues, despite the fact that female participation in various spheres was actively encouraged and promoted, they were not included in any major decision-making.

Despite these challenges, however, the Soviet commitment to address some of the challenges women faced created the ground for its self-described successful nature, which was far from the reality the majority of Central Asian women lived in. This is a rather important observation due to the fact that it has direct implications to the currently flourishing patriarchal gender ideology in the region.[43]

In other words, while the discussed Soviet efforts aimed at tackling women's issues have definitely produced some positive results, they have also contributed to the emergence and persistence of an interesting phenomenon in the former Soviet space. Overoptimistic evaluations of the Soviet-era policies regarding gender equality have partially shaped the current tendency in Central Asia to neglect women in designing development strategies and projects. Lazreg (2000), for instance, argues that these perceptions of post-Soviet reality have transformed gender inequality into somewhat of a nonproblem, which does not represent an issue "worthy of concern".[44] The myth that the Communist Party was generally able to achieve gender equality was built upon the fact that Soviet republics, indeed, witnessed certain progress in terms of higher participation of women in the workforce and an increased female representation in traditionally "male" industries. However, it becomes evident after a closer examination of the implemented policies that the regime did little to fundamentally transform traditional gender roles, especially in the Central Asian context. Regardless, the belief that men and women were treated equally under the communist rule persists to this day and often affects local gender and development initiatives. Hence, it is important to pay due attention to the unique history of post-Soviet states, such as Kazakhstan, and recognize the peculiarities of the context they emerged in, in order to understand its past and present perception of development.

Why Soviet History Matters for Kazakhstan's Aid Policy

The Soviet Union and the legacies of it's almost a century-long rule have played an important role in the development of Kazakhstan's foreign aid policies. To this day, Kazakhstan's official development assistance is distributed through several large-scale ODA projects, one of which is directed at assisting partner countries in the sphere of education.

In different stages of its development, the Republic of Kazakhstan provided humanitarian assistance to its Southern neighbors, mainly Kyrgyzstan, Tajikistan and Afghanistan, through the distribution of educational grants and construction of educational institutions. For instance, since 2006, Kazakhstan has delivered 22,263,445 US million worth of consumer goods as humanitarian aid to Tajikistan.[45]

In addition, an agreement between the Republic of Kazakhstan and the Islamic Republic of Afghanistan, under which 1000 Afghan students were to be trained at Kazakh higher education institutions, came into force back in 2010. Nazarbayev stated that the main goal of the efforts of the states involved in Afghanistan, including Kazakhstan, should be economic development of the region and not achievement of local military objectives.[46] In this light, Kazakhstan's education initiative, according to Nazarbayev, was specifically designed to address these challenges in the country (ibid.). Similar to the above-mentioned experience of Kazakhstan as a subject of the Soviet modernization project, Kazakhstan's current development assistance initiatives catered to its Southern partners mirror the Soviet approach.

More specifically, certain parallels can be drawn between Soviet efforts in Kazakh SSR and Kazakhstan's projects directed at Central Asia and Afghanistan. During the time of the USSR, the government has created educational opportunities for Kazakhs (and other non-Russians) through establishing the system of admission quotas ("sistema bronirovaniya mest") with the mission to assist Kazakhstan in its path of developing local national "intelligentsia" (well-educated class). Similarly, Kazakhstan as an ODA provider began its official operation in the region by introducing a system of educational grants for Afghan students who wish to pursue their higher education in Kazakhstani universities (mostly located in the major cities—the capital Nur-Sultan and the Southern financial capital Almaty). As it was discussed above, exchange programs catered to advanced students from Kazakhstan (and other non-Russian republics) were a common practice and offered an opportunity for the selected students to complete their education at the institutions in central cities of the USSR.

Later in 2018, the Ministry of Foreign Affairs of the Republic of Kazakhstan adopted another initiative within its ODA framework with the mission to offer foreign students an opportunity to receive high-quality training at one of the leading universities in Kazakhstan—Nazarbayev University (NU). It should be noted that, by analogy with the system set out by the Soviet regime, Kazakhstan has allocated a set number of admissions to the most prestigious university in Kazakhstan to the students from abroad. As a part of this initiative, foreign students from Central Asia (Kyrgyzstan, Tajikistan, Turkmenistan, Uzbekistan) and Afghanistan (for each country: undergraduate –1 place, magistracy –1 place, doctoral studies –1 place) were invited to apply to Nazarbayev University and obtain their education in any of the offered 17 undergraduate programs, 27 master's and doctoral programs during the 2018–2020 and 2018–2022 academic years. As of 2019, the country allocated the total of 15 special educational grants and reserved admissions to the students from the countries of Central Asia and Afghanistan.

What represents a point of particular importance is the fact that academic training at Nazarbayev University is conducted only in English. Due to the fact that the admission requirements at NU are very high, every year the best students from all over Kazakhstan, with a high level of training and highest test scores, apply to study at this university. In other words, the institution is considered a forge of elite cadres in Kazakhstan. As such, it is understood that applicants from the partner countries that fall under this scheme of Kazakhstan's ODA have sufficiently strong competencies, and most likely are not representatives of remote rural schools. More specifically, in order to prepare for admission to the university, applicants must be fluent in English and pass relevant examinations in English depending on the department's specific requirements (such as IELTS, SAT, GMAT, GRE). Such a process, which requires a lot of resources and time, points at the somewhat elitist approach of this ODA initiative.

Another type of offering education opportunity in the form of Kazakh development assistance is organization of educational seminars. For instance, within the framework of Kazakhstan's ODA project, Kazakhstan jointly with UNDP and the Embassy of Israel organized a special scientific and practical seminar targeting Central Asian agricultural workers. The seminar was titled "Improving the productivity and profitability of agribusiness through training farmers and agricultural specialists of Central Asian countries on innovative technologies for water and energy saving" and took place in Almaty on April 24–28, 2017.[47]

Among the attendees, there were farmers and agricultural experts from Kyrgyzstan, Tajikistan, Uzbekistan and Turkmenistan, as well as representatives of various testing commissions, practical water conservation experts, scientists, heads of the agricultural departments and leaders of the agricultural sector. During the training, participants were given lectures on the topic of advanced knowledge and methods in the use of Israeli drip irrigation technologies in crop production and had an opportunity to learn about Kazakhstan's experience of their practical implementation.

On top of that, the attendees participated in the discussion dedicated to the opportunities and challenges of integrated implementation of "green"/ecologically friendly approaches through adoption of the best adaptation technologies and practices. The training was offered by the invited specialists from Israel Yigal Meister and Yaakov Lev in cooperation with local Kazakhstani experts (NANOC and S. Seifullin Agrarian University). The event was held at the Ushkonyr Knowledge Distribution Center, where, with the support of the Israeli Embassy and the Israeli Agency MASHAV, a demonstration platform of advanced Israeli water-saving technologies has been in operation since 2015. Israel shared valuable knowledge with experts from Central Asia as one of the countries that managed to have successfully applied the revolutionary technology of drip irrigation and have gained significant experience in adapting this solution in arid and semi-arid climatic conditions.

During this seminar, representatives of the agribusiness of Kyrgyzstan, Tajikistan, Uzbekistan and Turkmenistan were not only presented with the necessary practical knowledge and skills, which they could apply at home, but also had the opportunity to share and exchange their insights on their most successful experiences in the field of effective agro-production using new technologies.

In the second half of the seminar that was held at the Arnasay knowledge dissemination center, which focuses on the practical use of 35 energy-efficient and water-saving technologies, project participants were introduced to the practical tips on promoting best practices in the field of economical water consumption, creating effective areas for growing organic products in closed ground, as well as in development of technologies of verma and aqua-cultivation. According to them, this event was a clear demonstration of a successful approach to spreading knowledge and information about the best agro-approaches in the development of modern efficient cooperative agro-production.

Speaking of initiatives for women empowerment, in July 2017, Kazakhstan in cooperation with UNDP and JICA organized a series of trainings for Afghan civil servants and non-governmental organization workers with the mission to assist them in enhancing their capacity. The project was a product of the conducted meeting between the First President of the Republic of Kazakhstan Nursultan Nazarbayev and the Premier Minister of Japan Shinzo Abe, which was held in Nur-Sultan in October 2015 during Abe's visit to Kazakhstan. During that meeting, the leaders of the two nations agreed to deepen and expand strategic partnership between the two countries, which was reflected in their Joint Statement.

A total of twenty-four Afghan representatives, working in the field of public administration, medicine and education, and nominated by the Ministry of Foreign Affairs of the Islamic Republic of Afghanistan attended the seminar with an intent to learn about Kazakhstan's development experience and gained knowledge and expertise in those areas. The participants of the seminar paid visits to the Center for Population Services in Nur-Sultan in order to familiarize themselves with the Kazakhstani single-window system. Moreover, the event also incorporated a cultural program. The training was also conducted of Kazakhstan's larger ODA engagement with Afghanistan aimed at strengthening the economic independence of Afghan women.[48]

In April 2018, the project entered the next stage when the second seminar, which was designed for specialists from Afghanistan and dedicated to the topics of maternal and child health care, took place at Nazarbayev University (NU) in Nur-Sultan, Kazakhstan. NU joined the project as one of the main partners in its implementation (data provided during an interview with the author at the Ministry of Foreign Affairs). The budget of the project was funded by the UNDP-Japan Partnership Fund, while Kazakhstan's involvement was in the form of technical assistance, specifically, through the transfer of experience and knowledge.[49]

Notes

1. Escobar, A. (1995). *Encountering development: The making and unmaking of the Third World* (1st ed.). Princeton: Princeton University Press.
2. See Falkingam (1999).
3. Charman, K. (2007). Kazakhstan: A state-led liberalized market economy. In D. Lane & M. Myant (Eds.), *Varieties of capitalism in post-communist countries*. Palgrave; Myant, M., & Drahokoupil, J. (2008). International integration and the structure of exports in Central Asian republics. *Eurasian Geography and Economics, 49*(5), 604–622.
4. Akiner (1997), Beissinger and Young (2002), and Ishkanian (2004).
5. Falkingham (1999) and Pomfret (2010).
6. For example, Martha Brill Olcott (1995). The Kazakhs. *Studies of Nationalities*. Hoover Institution Press (Appendix 2).
7. Kazakhskyi kraevoi komitet RKP (b)—VKP (b) (Kazraikom RKP(b)—VKP(b)), Agitatsionno-propagandistskiy otdel, "Protokol

krayev. konferenciy po rabochemu i krestyanskomu obrazovaniyu" fond 141, opis 1, ed. Kr. №1525, 1927 god, na 506 listah (p. 6).

8. Kazakhskyi kraevoi komitet RKP (b)—VKP (b) (Kazraikom RKP(b)—VKP(b)), Agitatsionno-propaganditskiy otdel, gorod Kyzyl-Orda, "Materialy o rabote agit.prop.otdela Kazaraikoma RKP (b). Dokladnye: o gramotnosti kazakhskogo naseleniya i dr. Istoricheskie spravki, protokoly agit.prop." fond 141, opis 1, ed. Kr. №336, 1925 god, na 47 listah (p. 10).
9. "Protokol krayev. konferenciy po rabochemu i krestyanskomu obrazovaniyu", p. 6.
10. Until 1925, Kazakhs were officially referred to as Kirgiz.
11. Kazakh village.
12. Main Political and Educational Committee.
13. "Protokol krayev. konferenciy po rabochemu i krestyanskomu obrazovaniyu", p. 7.
14. Kazakhskyi kraevoi komitet RKP (b)—VKP (b) (Kazraikom RKP(b)—VKP(b)), Agitatsionno-propaganditskiy otdel, gorod Kyzyl-Orda (p. 7).
15. Bilinsky, Y. (1968). Education of the non-Russian peoples in the USSR, 1917–1967, an essay. *Slavic Review, 27*(3), 411–437.
16. Kazakhskyi kraevoi komitet RKP (b)—VKP (b) (Kazraikom RKP(b)—VKP(b)), Agitatsionno-propaganditskiy otdel, gorod Kyzyl-Orda, (document #016).
17. For instance, Ahn et al. (2018).
18. Bilinsky (1968).
19. Natsional'naya politika VKPb. https://archive.org/details/natsionalnaia_politika_vkpb_1930/page/n145.
20. DeWitt, N. (1961). *Education and professional employment in the U.S.S.R.* National Science Foundation.
21. Bilinsky (1968, p. 427).
22. Istoriya SSSR. (1971). *Izdatel'stvo Akademii Nauk SSSR.* Izdatel'stvo Nauka. https://play.google.com/books/reader?id=ufXTAAAAMAAJ&hl=ru&pg=GBS.PA5.
23. Bilinsky (1968, p. 428).
24. Kazakhskyi kraevoi komitet RKP (b)—VKP (b) (Kazraikom RKP(b)—VKP(b)), Agitatsionno-propaganditskiy otdel, gorod Kyzyl-Orda, (pp. 7–9).
25. "Protokol krayev. konferenciy po rabochemu i krestyanskomu obrazovaniyu", p. 25.

26. Ibid., p. 30.
27. Ibid., p. 20.
28. Tsentraln'nyi Komitet KP(b) Kazakhstana, gor. Alma-Ata, Sel'skohozyaistvennyi sektor podgotovki sel'skozyaistvennyh kadrov, Ukazaniya TSKKP (b) Kazakhstana, dokladnye zapiski otdela, obkomov partii, narkomatov sovkhozov i semledeliya Kazakhskoi SSR ob obespechenii mekhanizatorskimi kadrami i podgotovki massovoy kvalifikatsii dlya sel'skogo hozyaistva, fund 708, opis' 411, №1217, na 78 listah, 1940—"Svodnaya ot 1939 goda", p. 38.
29. Racioppi and See (1995, p. 175).
30. Tsentralnyi Komitet KP(b) Kazakhstana, gor. Alma-Ata, Otdel rukovodyashchih partiynyh organov Zhensektor, "Dokladnye zapiski i spravki obkomov i raikomov KP(b) Kazakhstana o realizatsii resheniy II syezda partii po rabote sredi zhenshchin, Spiski zhenshchin, vydvinutyh na otvetstvennye raboty" fond 708, opis 2/1, ed. Kr. №649, 1938 god, na 165 listah (Doklad k soveshchaniyu instruktorov po rabote sredi zhenshchin, document #101, p. 143).
31. Rasnake et al. (2000).
32. Despite the official prohibition, in reality, such practices persisted.
33. Kazakhskyi kraevoi komitet RKP (b)—VKP (b) (Kazraikom RKP(b)—VKP(b)), Organizatsionno-raspredelitelnyi informats. Stat. protdel, "Obzory, spravki, svodki o sostoyanii i rabote Uralskogo Aktubinskogo i Akmolinskogo Gubkomov VKP(b) Kustanaiskogo okruzhkoma i Kara0kalpakskogo obkoma VKP(b) i o rabote sredi zhenshchin KSSR," fond 141, opis 1, ed. Kr. №697, 1926 god, na 165 listah (p. 14, document #068).
34. Kazakhskyi kraevoi komitet RKP (b)—VKP (b) (Kazraikom RKP(b)—VKP(b)), Otdel Rabotnits i krestyan, gorod Kyzyl-Orda, "Materialy po voprosu zhenskogo obrazovaniya v Kazakhstane. Materialy o vovlechenii zhenshchin v shkoly, VUZy, Vtuzy, Komvuzy, kluby, krasnye usoiki i td. Svodki o rabote delegatskih sobraniy i dr. za 1928," fond 141, opis 1, ed. Kr. №2370, 1928 god, na 69 listah (document #062).
35. Buckley, M. (1989). *Soviet interpretations of the woman question*. University of Michigan Press.
36. Kazakhskyi kraevoi komitet RKP (b)—VKP (b) (Kazraikom RKP(b)—VKP(b)), Otdel Rabotnits i krestyanok, "Material, tezisy,

programy dlya zhen.kursov po vprosam o vozniknovenii soyuza koshchi, KSSR, po ohrane mat., zemleustroistve, zhivotnovodstve i po antireligioznoi rabote," fond 141, opis 1, ed. Hr. #1607, 1927 god, na 63 listah (pp. 1–3).
37. Kazakhskyi kraevoi komitet RKP (b)—VKP (b) (Kazraikom RKP(b)—VKP(b)), Otdel Rabotnits i krestyan, gorod Kyzyl-Orda.
38. Wood (1997).
39. Primary data obtained by the author
40. Racioppi and Sea (1995).
41. Buckley, M. (1989). *Soviet interpretations of the woman question*. University of Michigan Press; Lapidus, G. W. (1978). *Women in Soviet society*. University of California Press.
42. Gal, S., & Kligman, G. (2000). *Politics of gender after socialism*. Princeton University Press.
43. Buckley, M. (1989). *Soviet Interpretations of the woman question*. University of Michigan Press; Lapidus, G. W. (1978). *Women in Soviet society*. University of California Press.
44. Moghadam (2000, p. 26).
45. Lazreg (2000).
46. Interview 4, 2018.
47. Nazarbayev, N. (2010, November 2). Nursultan Nazarbayev: V nashei druzhbe net nikakih sekretov with Vasilyev, A./ Interviewer. *Rossiyskaya Gazeta*.
48. Interview 1, 2017.
49. Insebayeva (Forthcoming).

CHAPTER 6

In the Colonial Matrix of Power: The Aftermath of the Soviet Collapse

Abstract This chapter turns to discussing Kazakhstan's experience as a foreign aid recipient in the years following its independence and its transition into an ODA donor. Over the years, Kazakhstan has transitioned from a recipient of Moscow's donations under the Soviet rule to a benefactor of Western development aid in the 1990s. Given Kazakhstan's unique experiences as a constituent and independent republic, a foreign aid recipient and an aid provider, this chapter will argue that international donors have played a significant role in shaping Kazakhstan's development path and have impacted its policy choices regarding its foreign aid activities. More specifically, the study argues that the Western aid has majorly influenced Kazakhstan's own development strategy during the 2000s, and, subsequently, its foreign aid policy in early 2010s. In particular, the discussion in the first part of this chapter emphasizes the link between knowledge acquired by the Kazakh leadership at different stages of the state's development and policies that the Kazakh government has eventually produced. The discussion provides a brief explanation of Kazakhstan's decision to cut its dependence on foreign aid in the early 2000s and to adhere to the self-reliance principle, which the Western donorship has been an important determinant of. This section will explain how international factors have influenced Kazakhstan's current ODA system.

N. Insebayeva, *Modernity, Development and Decolonization of Knowledge in Central Asia*, Politics and History in Central Asia,
https://doi.org/10.1007/978-981-16-5117-5_6

Keywords Post-Cold War · Transition · Nazarbayev · Self-reliance · Paris Declaration

As shown by the discussion in Chapter 5, Kazakhstan was subject to the peculiar Soviet modernization project driven by socialist ideals and has been isolated from virtually any other external influences for almost a century.[1] After the collapse of this Communist bubble, however, the former USSR countries joined an open, market-based international order as newly independent states. Therefore, Kazakhstan, along with other post-socialist republics, was required to make a drastic transition from their Soviet past to new institutions and rules in order to fit into the global system. While there exist many other instances of past colonies and dependent territories that have since gained their independence, there has also been a tendency among these nations to follow the model of statehood brought to them by their colonizers. Contrary to this, Kazakhstan embarked upon a path of development, which demanded its fundamental transformation and restructuring. The very foundation of Kazakhstan's statehood at the time, i.e., the socialist ideology and economic model set out by the Soviet regime, has collapsed, leaving the country no choice but to adapt to the world led by globalization and transnational capitalism.

The environment Kazakhstan found itself in shifted from maximum isolation from everything non-Soviet to overwhelming global intervention and engagement.[2] In the post-Cold War context, various external actors, such as foreign governments and international organizations that possessed more resources and power, have become actively involved in the state-building process in Central Asia.[3]

In other words, the collapse of the USSR, which has left the former Soviet republics in the ruins of the communist era, marked the starting point of substantial international presence in Central Asia in the form of development assistance programs. The end of communism and the newly found independence meant that the post-Soviet countries had to transition from central planning to free market economies and were expected to adopt principles of democratic governance. As new actors entered the development arena, the big foreign aid players, such as the USA and the countries-members of the OECD, officially commenced their development assistance contributions in the region.

However, aid often came with a list of conditions and requirements, which recipients ought to meet.[4] For instance, Western assistance providers sometimes mandated institutional and legislative changes in the recipient states—the requirements that were attached to their interest loans. Due to this donor practice of utilizing foreign aid as a political tool, aid negotiations pertaining to the condition and requirements of aid became a crucial part of development assistance. This gave donors political and economic leverage, which at times could be argued to have potentially undermined autonomous decision-making in the recipient states.[5]

The dominant narrative in the relevant academic literature on development assistance and negotiations was that the country with the biggest bargaining power does best at the negotiation table.[6] Donor-countries that tend to have more economic resources and political power, unsurprisingly, fit into this criterion. Although donors adopted different approaches to development assistance, including how they choose to deal with recipients, one of the biggest challenges of this donor-recipient dynamic was the lack of recipient country's involvement in project identification, design and evaluation.[7] As argued by Jones (1993) and Samoff (1990), some donors exhibited limited concern for the recipient's self-formulated priorities and needs, which led to the implementation of "unwanted projects", disempowered local decision-makers and undermined development of local expertise.

In other words, it was argued that many development projects designed by foreign funding agencies were based on their own understanding and analysis of the state of affairs in the recipient states without a careful consideration for the local culture and knowledge. As most of the work pertaining to the delivery of development assistance was also conducted by the donor side, there was a risk of aid dependency, resentment and passive position among recipients.[8]

Hence, the prevalence of donor dominance in decision-making and project design during that time has led many to conclude that it undermined the very purpose of aid in building local human capital and recipient's future self-sustainability. As such, a general consensus was that the success of development assistance efforts is directly linked to effective policy dialogue between donors and recipients.[9]

Kazakhstan, along with other four Central Asian states—Uzbekistan, Kyrgyzstan, Tajikistan and Turkmenistan, was added to the list of ODA recipients created by DAC in 1992—soon after gaining its independence in 1991.[10]

Kazakhstan has quickly become the recipient of rather large amounts of US bilateral aid. For instance, according to the data provided by the State Department (2002), during the 10 years of Kazakhstan's independence, the country has received $874.3 million in American development assistance. Moreover, having entered a period of uncertainty, Central Asian states started to engage with various international financial institutions such as the International Monetary Fund (IMF), the World Bank and Asian Development Bank, which could offer help in the form of aid in exchange for implementation of a string of neoliberal education reforms. This, of course, should be seen as a part of the larger picture, where foreign aid has been used by the "traditional" donors as a tool to advance institutional transformation and promote certain (neoliberal) values in developing states.

Many of the donors that operated in the region provided significant resources in the form of technical assistance aimed at institution-building and promotion of secondary and higher education. Although these actors have engaged in various development assistance programs and projects in Kazakhstan starting from the early 1990s, there was a lack of official structure for foreign aid coordination in Kazakhstan. Hence, there were many instances when different governmental and non-governmental bodies approached potential donors directly, which makes it difficult to assess all externally funded development programs implemented in Kazakhstan in detail.

The situation has slightly changed when in 1992, Nazarbayev issued a decree to establish the National Agency for Foreign Investment (NAFI)[11]—the body responsible for attracting international donors, negotiating priority areas and producing feasibility assessments of proposed initiatives. However, due to the government's lack of experience in dealing with a variety of funding agencies, aid coordination remained unsystematic. The Agency was later reorganized into the Committee on External Loans under the Ministry of Finance of the Republic of Kazakhstan, which was responsible for monitoring and managing governmental and non-governmental loans. Another body—the National Agency for Strategic Development assumed the responsibility of coordinating and monitoring of a different type of assistance—foreign grants. The system of aid coordination continued to experience certain changes throughout the years, which contributed to the persistence of further challenges pertaining to aid coordination and project duplication.

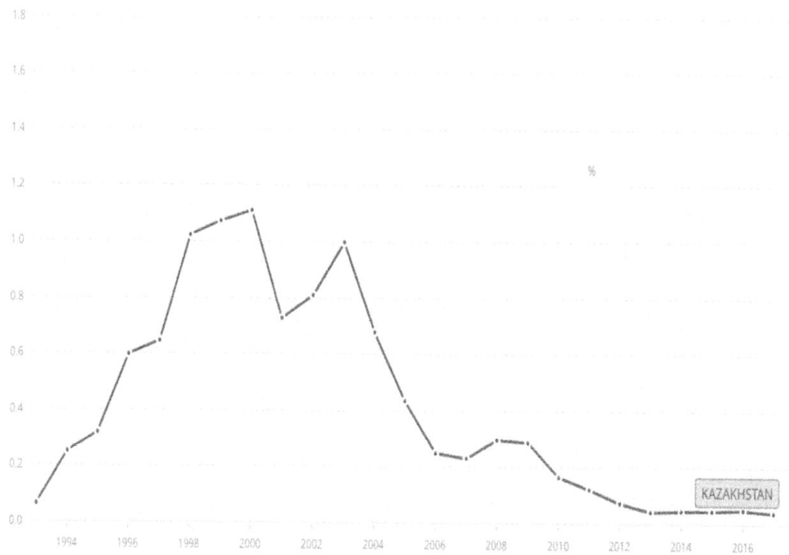

Graph 6.1 Net official development assistance received (% of GNI) Kazakhstan (1993–2017) (*Source* The World Bank national accounts data, 2019)

Despite great amount of international attention and development assistance, however, the costs of such international pressure on the part of the donors were not offset by the expected benefits in the form of a sharp economic boost. Hence, in October 2000, following a deep economic shock, President Nazarbayev presented his annual Address to the People of Kazakhstan, in which he emphasized how important it was for Kazakhstan to cut its dependency on foreign aid. It was announced that the number of short-term loans and aid, in general, accepted by the country from foreign donors would undergo significant cuts; according to the new vision, the country was to finance domestic reforms with its "own" money. With the appropriate reforms that followed this announcement, Kazakhstan was relatively soon to become the most donor-independent state in the region with international actors, in the form of financial institutions and aid agencies, having less influence over the Kazakhstani government in this respect.

Such policy reorientation is reflected in the data on ODA provided both by the World Bank (Graph 6.1), which draws on the net ODA received by Kazakhstan as a percentage of the country's Gross National Income (GNI). What this graph is designed to capture is states' dependency on aid over time. Despite some relatively significant fluctuations observed between 2002–2004 and 2007–2008 (which could potentially be explained by the domestic political crisis of 2001–2002 and the global financial crisis, respectively), Kazakhstan's dependency on official development assistance has been decreasing since the beginning of the twenty-first century—a time when the government shifted toward the discussed foreign policy re-orientation—the principle of "self-reliance".

On February 28, 2007, in his Address to the People of the Republic of Kazakhstan, Nazarbayev stressed the progress the country had made, and once again expressed the commitment of the state to continue to follow its self-reliance principle and to continue efforts toward the establishment of a knowledge-based economy by investing into human capital. In other words, instead of referring to the international expertise, Kazakhstan was said to be determined to build a pool of local professionals, which the national economy was to rely on in the future:

> "We (Kazakhstan) have built a strong foundation for our economy and statehood. We have entered a radically new stage of our development.
>
> We have achieved domestic stability in the country, managed to create a strong basis for social development, and built the strongest economy in the region. Kazakhstan is no longer a Third World country - this is the main result of our work over the past decade…
>
> Almost all successful modern states that are actively integrated in the international economic system have relied on the principle of "smart economy". To create this, we need to focus on developing our own human capital".

Through invoking Kazakhstan's history, this discussion aims to emphasize that Kazakhstan's identity as an aid recipient has contributed to its understanding of what foreign aid is, how aid strategies are to be designed and how aid is to be practiced.

> "Kazakhstan's experience as a former recipient-state has undoubtedly influenced our current development cooperation policy. Firstly, it is worth noting the experience of international donors during the time they operated in Kazakhstan. We seriously analyzed their approach - what worked for them, what did not work, how they built a dialogue with our government. Secondly, we analyzed our reaction to the activities of international

donors. For example, what we were interested in, what mistakes we have made. Based on our experience as a former recipient country, we perfectly understand how our partner countries feel and how they view assistance".[12]

Moreover, it can be argued that Kazakhstan's experience as an aid recipient contributed to the fact that Kazakhstan, as a donor, does not attempt to instruct partner countries on how to develop through imposing conditionality, which distinguishes it from the traditional donors.

The latter have been known for the aid paradigm, which is premised on an inherently hierarchical relationship between donors and recipients. Kazakhstan, on the other hand, supports the development path chosen by its partner countries, which is based on their "national interests, partnership with Kazakhstan and international environment".[13] The country stands by an "individual approach that takes into account political, economic, social and national characteristics of each recipient state".[14] As it was mentioned earlier, within the framework of its development assistance, Kazakhstan has implemented an education project involving 1,000 students from Afghanistan for the purpose of fostering the state's development. Importantly, the selected disciplines offered as a part of this program do not exclusively feature the ones proposed by Kazakhstan, rather the education initiative is designed to meet the needs and interests of the recipient and covers fields of specialization offered by the Afghan side with a consideration of Kazakhstan's capabilities.[15]

Therefore, Kazakhstan, as a former aid recipient and simultaneously a foreign aid provider, significantly differs from the Western donors in this respect—instead of introducing conditionality on its aid, the country focuses on assisting the recipient countries in building up their economic capacity.[16] This mirrors Kazakhstan's own development trajectory, which is based on the official slogan "Economy first, then politics". President Nazarbayev has emphasized on multiple occasions that political instability is something the country should always strive to avoid, while economic growth ought to be the focus of the nation's development. Kazakhstan's understanding of a successful development path is, thus, "built around the ideas of a strong independent state, stability, economic development and technocratic rationality".[17]

Such focus on fostering "self-reliance" in recipient countries once again serves as a reflection of Kazakhstan's identity as a former aid recipient, and its formed values and beliefs, which the country announced back in

2000. For instance, while addressing the people of Kyrgyzstan, President Nazarbayev advised Kazakhstan's neighbors to stop relying on international assistance and loans and to start "working more".[18] Afghanistan has received a similar message, which stated that "the country should rely on its own strength; It is impossible to assure sustainable growth of the state relying on humanitarian aid and loans".[19]

The experience of being an aid recipient as well as Kazakhstan's choice in favor of knowledge-based development has ultimately affected the country's foreign aid policy and aid patterns later on when the state became a donor itself.

Thus, Kazakhstan's identity as an aid recipient has shaped its understanding of what foreign aid is, how aid strategies are to be designed and how aid is to be distributed. Having realized the drawbacks of aid dependency, which come in the form of political and economic pressures, Kazakhstan's reluctance to rely too heavily on loans and foreign aid providers has led to its determinacy to promote self-reliance. This principle has ultimately affected the country's foreign aid policy choices later on when the state became a donor itself.

International Factors

Although Kazakhstan shares some similarities with the "emerging" Southern donor group, Kazakhstan also aims to contribute to the development of the established aid regime through compliance with particular international norms and standards embraced by the DAC donor group. For instance, DAC recommendations on aid institutions postulate: (1) aid institutions should be integrated, (2) donors should have a legal framework governing their ODA in the form of a comprehensive ODA Act which defines overall aid purposes, strategies and policies and (3) aid should have performance monitoring and evaluation systems.[20]

As such, in 2013, in accordance with DAC standards, Kazakhstan has announced its commitment to transition into a development assistance donor and has introduced the ODA Concept of the Republic of Kazakhstan—the document ought to set the roadmap of the state's development aid initiative.

The same year, as it was mentioned in the previous chapter, the government adopted the Law of the Republic of Kazakhstan on Official Development Assistance.

In addition, the adoption of principle of "reducing the number of duplicative ODA programs" and "coordinating Kazakhstan's assistance measures with activities of other bilateral and multilateral donors"[21] can also be reflective of Kazakhstan's motivation to meet international norms and standards.[22] To the international foreign aid community division of labor or complementarity has been a vital approach since 2005 that played an important role in achieving one of the main principles of the Paris Declaration—donor harmonization. Such a strategy calls for the identification of the donor's respective comparative advantages, which would then serve as the basis for global collaborative effort toward more division of labor and complementarity in the world aid architecture.[23] It is also worth mentioning that a set of principles mentioned in the official documents on Kazakhstan's foreign aid resonate with the Busan Partnership agreement that specifically highlights a set of common principles for all development actors, which are key to making development cooperation effective: focus on results, partnerships for development, transparency and shared responsibility, ownership.

Furthermore, Kazakhstan believes that development of technological capabilities, as well as human and institutional capacity, are essential preconditions for growth. Therefore, the country stresses the principal source of its comparative advantage—its technical and organizational knowledge, which it has accumulated throughout the years of independence. Thus, in line with DAC standards, Kazakhstan pays significant attention to social sectors to promote growth and development in beneficiary countries.

Kazakhstan's 2015 decision to deliver development assistance to countries of Africa, Oceania and the Caribbean through its contributions to local capacity building in terms of training for young professionals is another illustration of the country's commitment to DAC principles. In 2015, Kazakhstan implemented the AFRICANA project aimed at developing a positive image of the country in the recipient states, as well as at building and strengthening professional capacity of the participants (mid-career professionals, graduates, researchers) through organizing trainings for specialists in the fields of oil and gas exploration, public health care and agriculture from 23 African states.[23]

The provided discussion shows the country's aspirations at following certain norms set by the traditional aid providers.

As noted in the previous sections of this study, domestic factors, such as historical experiences and domestic politics, have played an important role in constructing Kazakhstan's donor identity and its interests.

However, the behaviors of foreign aid donors are also heavily influenced by shared expectations and norms regarding development assistance that are constructed and reconstructed at the international level. As such, external ideational and social pressures legitimize or constrain aid practices pursued by the providers of foreign aid. Accordingly, "states and state elites' fashion a political self or identity in relation to the international community" and seek "legitimization, conformity and esteem".[25]

Kazakhstan has continuously explained its aspirations to become a development donor through the prism of the importance of this role in building the "belt of good- neighborliness" around Kazakhstan's borders, which requires the country to create and maintain its positive international image, follow its multi-vector foreign policy approach, ensure economic development and increase its political authority in the international community. Kazakhstan's active foreign policy choice and its determination to be an active participant in the global negotiations on the most prominent issues have been dictated by its dedication to ensure its security through membership in various international organizations, which Kazakhstan sees not only as a symbol of international recognition, but also as an alternative security practice (ibid.). In other words, Kazakhstan believes that its success at ensuring its positive international reputation and being an active and prominent member of the international community is a good indicator of the country's ability to ensure its survival.

It is important to note that in the official discourse Kazakhstani aid is primarily framed as a foreign policy tool rather than "charity" or moral obligation. Kazakhstan's past as a recipient, who has experienced the efforts by the Western powers to advance domestic neoliberal transformation, contributes to how the state defines and uses its own ODA at the present time. Diplomatic use of Kazakhstan's aid has a clearly strategic edge in procuring Kazakhstan's national security.

The strategic motivations behind Kazakh aid become evident from the fact that Kazakhstan's ODA assigns a particular importance to Central Asia and its own commitment to contribute to the "stabilization of socio-economic and political environment in partner- states; prevention of illegal migration; fight against terrorism and extremism, and the formation of the belt of good-neighborliness".[26] This indicates that Kazakhstan aims to use its ODA and other programs to secure their leading position in the region and cultivate strategic linkages with the states of a significant strategic importance. In this light, Central Asia plays a prominent role in Kazakhstan's foreign policy due to the role the stable regional environment plays in the country's own economic development. Providing aid to the neighbors, in this sense, contributes to the establishment and maintenance of friendly relations for the purpose of creating more trade and investment opportunities, and most importantly, fosters growth and prevents instability both in the recipient states and the region as a whole.

Stressing that Kazakh aid flows have been reflective of Kazakhstan's diplomatic needs mainly through generating goodwill, cultivating good relations and building the country's image as ready to provide support and assistance to its regional and international "friends" is the main strategy Kazakhstan has been actively utilizing in its attempts to justify such expenditure decisions amidst recent national budget cuts at home. The officials emphasize the progress Kazakhstan has made so far as an upper middle-income state, through which they aim to distance themselves from the status of a recipient and legitimize the introduction of the costly development aid initiatives. Kazakhstan's aid discourse does not downplay the fact that the national foreign aid flows and projects are primarily driven by Kazakhstan's own national interests, while also serving possible interests and needs of the recipient countries.

Back in 2007, Kazakhstan first declared its preparedness and commitment to put forward its bid for a non-permanent member seat for the term 2011–2012 (UN, 2007) on one of the global community's most important institutions—United Nations Security Council (UNSC), but later withdrew its candidacy in favor of India (UN, 2010). In 2014, the country went through with the initial plan and campaigned again to get the seat in 2017–2018 (Kazakhstan's UN bid, 2017). Kazakhstan grounded its bid on four priority areas for international cooperation: food, water, energy and nuclear security. In 2016, the campaign has been proven successful after Kazakhstan beat Thailand during the election at the plenary session of the UN General Assembly obtaining 138 votes out of the total 193 (Kazakhstan secures seat, 2016). Thus, Kazakhstan has become the first Central Asian state to be elected to the UNSC. Then Chairman of the Mazhilisof the Parliament of the Republic of Kazakhstan Dzhakupov (2015) stressed that Kazakhstan's ODA and humanitarian aid efforts directed at its partners have played an important role in the country's ability to win over the necessary votes.

On top of that, international experts have long discussed the importance of Africa as an international aid recipient and criticized many donors for not adequately engaging with the continent (Premature donors,

2013). Thus, Africa has officially become another important destination for Kazakhstan's foreign aid.[27] In addition to obtaining and cultivating new markets, aid to Africa shows Kazakhstan's ability and commitment to behave responsibly in addressing key challenges of the developing world. Having experienced difficulties as a landlocked country itself, Kazakhstan is interested in addressing the challenges that limit potential growth of the fifteen landlocked African countries. Kazakhstan's position opposite its other landlocked counterparts creates great opportunities for expanding the state's South-South and Triangular Co-operation with these partners.[28]

"Africa is a continent of opportunities which is being actively explored by economic giants such as China, India and the Western states, and it is those opportunities that Kazakhstan intends to develop in cooperation with our African partners. Our country is interested in establishing closer relations of mutually beneficial political, economic and trade cooperation with African countries"—said Former Foreign Minister Idrissov.[29] Importantly, official on-the-ground regional presence in Africa, which the country currently lacks, could be facilitated with the help of the UNDP, which has already partnered up with Kazakhstan to implement the AFRICANA project, as mentioned by Helen Clark.[30]

As of now Kazakhstan focuses on contributing to the development of Africa through the experience exchange. As such, Nazarbayev University hosted an international seminar on public health for 24 specialists from 7 African states, during which expert from the Centre for Life Sciences and National Laboratory in Nur-Sultan addressed the most prominent issues in the fields of epidemiology, biomedicine and public health.[31] Moreover, in October 2015, an international seminar held at the Technical High School APEC Petrotechnic brought together local Kazakhstani experts and professionals from Africa to provide the latter with training in oil and gas business. Finally, the leading training center of the Atyrau region12 organized a series of lectures and workshops for 19 specialists from 7 African states, who got an opportunity to interact with the leading Kazakhstan oil and gas experts and visit the leading Kazakhstani corporations for the purpose of exploring modern methods and technologies of geological exploration, production, oil refining and transportation.[32]

Kazakhstan's interest in the African continent has been apparent from its consistent engagement with the region through multilateral and bilateral channels of Kazakh aid distribution. In 2011, Kazakhstan, "being a responsible member of the Organization of Islamic Cooperation (OIC) and chairing the OIC Council of Foreign Ministers" donated US$500,000 to Somalia to combat humanitarian crisis in the country caused by the devastating drought in East Africa.[33] Kazakhstan's engagement in the continent can be reflected in other instances when the state offered its help in the form of humanitarian aid. For example, in October 2014, Kazakhstan transferred the total of US$300,000 to the UNDP trust fund and the African Union to be used in the fight against Ebola virus.[34]

Kazakhstan has been proactively working on establishing diplomatic relations with the continent as well. For instance, the country joined the African Union as an observer-state, and opened its embassy in Addis Ababa, Ethiopia in 2013 and 2014, respectively. Moreover, the UNDP and Kazakhstan signed a cost-sharing agreement to help African continent to reach Sustainable Development Goals, according to which Kazakhstan is to provide technical support for any relevant institutions.[35]

To sum up, another fundamental characteristic of Kazakhstan's aid strategy is that it is not only influenced by its identity as a recipient, but that its framework is also shaped by the international discourses of official development assistance—a fact that is reflected in the principles and goals of Kazakhstan's ODA.

Notes

1. Akiner (1997).
2. Luong (2004, p. 2).
3. Luong (2004), Mendelson and Glenn (2002), and Weingthal (2002, 2004).
4. Carey (2007).
5. Eldstrom (1990).
6. Zartman (1985).
7. Hurst (1981).
8. Hurst (1983).
9. Cassen and Associated (1986).
10. History of DAC Lists of aid recipient countries (n.d.).
11. Ukaz Prezidenta Respubliki Kazakhstan N799. (1992, June 8). O sozdanii agentstva po inostrannym investitsiyam.
12. Interview 3, 2018.
13. Decree 415, 2014.

14. Concept of the Republic of Kazakhstan in the sphere of official development assistance. (2013). *Government of the Republic of Kazakhstan*.
15. Qazaqstan (2015) and Qazaqstan (2016).
16. Concept of the Republic of Kazakhstan in the sphere of official development assistance. (2013). *Government of the Republic of Kazakhstan*.
17. Insebayeva (2016).
18. Nursultan Nazarbayev (2012).
19. Kazakhstan prodolzhit pomogat Afghanistanu. (2010, December 3). *Tengrinews*.
20. OECD (2008).
21. Concept of the Republic of Kazakhstan in the sphere of official development assistance. (2013). *Government of the Republic of Kazakhstan*.
22. Law on Official Development Assistance (2014).
23. Division of labour, 2010.
24. UNDP. (2017). AFRICANA project brief.
25. Finnemore and Sikkink (1998, p. 902).
26. Concept of the Republic of Kazakhstan in the sphere of official development assistance. (2013). *Government of the Republic of Kazakhstan*.
27. Decree 415, 2017.
28. Clark, H. (2015, May 21). *Speech at the Astana Economic Forum on "Africa: The next driver of the global economy"*.
29. Orazgaliyeva, M. (2014, October 31). Kazakhstan's Official Development Assistance to focus on Central Asia, Afghanistan, says FM. *Astana Times*.
30. Witte (2015).
31. Kazakhstan podelilsya opytom so specialistami iz afrikanskogo kontinenta. (2015, August 4). *UNDP*.
32. Vstrechaem gostei iz Afriki! (2015, October 22). *Zhasatyrau*.
33. Kazakhstan to render aid to hungry people of Somalia. (2011, August 9), *Tengrinews.kz*.
34. Orazgaliyeva, M. (2014, October 31). Kazakhstan's Official Development Assistance to focus on Central Asia, Afghanistan, says FM. *Astana Times*.
35. Turebekova, A. (2015, June 26). Czech development cooperation experience could be useful for KazAID. *Astana Times*.

CHAPTER 7

Conclusion

Abstract This chapter summarizes the discussion provided in the previous chapters and points at the afore-mentioned gaps in existing literature, which is mainly rooted in rationalist understanding of aid. This chapter reiterates that Kazakhstan's case does not fit into the existing binary categorization of aid donors, i.e. "old"/Northern and "new"/Southern. It highlights that Kazakhstan stands as an "outlier", falling outside any of these groups due to its historical experiences.

Keywords Development aid provider · KazAID · Outlier · Southern identity · Northern "Others"

This book has set out to explore the transformation of Kazakhstan from a recipient country to a development aid provider. Kazakhstan became the first official development assistance (ODA) provider in the Central Asian region in December 2014 after adopting a series of relevant laws and announcing the decision to establish the Kazakhstan Agency for International Development (KazAID), thereby becoming an object of academic inquiry. To date, however, most scholarly works on the subject have been limited to exploring what strategic objectives Kazakhstan sets for itself embarking upon the path of an official development donor. As

N. Insebayeva, *Modernity, Development and Decolonization of Knowledge in Central Asia*, Politics and History in Central Asia,
https://doi.org/10.1007/978-981-16-5117-5_7

such, most studies in the field argue that Kazakh foreign aid practices are primarily driven by economic, political and strategic motivations of the current regime. This emphasis on motives for Kazakh aid in the relevant literature is not surprising and can be explained by the dominant conceptualization of foreign aid as a versatile policy tool utilized to deliver symbolic and practical gains to the donor states. As a result, most of these studies are rooted in rationalist understanding of the concept and remain preoccupied with analyzing how Kazakhstan pursues its interest strategically as a self-interested rational actor, rather than inquire where those interests and preferences come from. Thus, while it is important to acknowledge the contribution made by this useful research on the motivations that fuel Kazakhstan's aid-giving aspirations, it must also be recognized that to this day there is little knowledge about how Kazakhstan has emerged as a development cooperation provider, and most importantly what kind of new development actor Kazakhstan has become. The questions concerning norms, values, discourses and practices surrounding Kazakh donor activities remain unanswered, and the reasons behind the adoption of these particular characteristics and their emergence are left unexplored. This book attempted to offer some answers to these fundamental questions.

Drawing on the fieldwork in Nur-Sultan and Almaty (Kazakhstan) between 2016 and 2019, this study reveals that Kazakhstan as a foreign aid provider has embraced an identity that combines features and characteristics pertaining to both—emerging and traditional donors. On the one hand, it discursively constructed its identity as a "development cooperation partner", adopting the relevant discourse of mutual benefit, respect for sovereignty and non-interference, which places it among those donor states that actively associate themselves with the community of "emerging donors". On the other hand, Kazakhstan, as an aid provider, shared certain features that are usually associated with the traditional or "Northern" donor camp.

By focusing on Kazakhstan as a non-first tier provider this work made an attempt to expose a number of existing conceptual and theoretical problems that currently exist in the field of international development. In particular, despite the fact that over the past several decades, the existing international aid community has witnessed the emergence of a wide variety of new donors that adopt various approaches to and understandings of development assistance, their entry into the ranks of foreign aid providers was usually classified according to a predetermined system of categorizations. In particular, the arrival of a new group of actors is often met with an overarching label of "emerging donors", "Non-DAC donors" and "Southern donors".

In the relevant literature, this terminology is commonly used to separate the emergence of new actors from the perceived "development regime" established by traditional donors or designate these new actors to a place that is different from the imaginary space occupied by the members of the Organization for Economic Cooperation and Development (OECD) DAC Committee. The existing aid and development scholarship has noted that the classification or categorization of new providers as "new" or "emerging" is not entirely correct, since some providers in this group of "new" donors are not novices when it comes to the provision of foreign assistance, which is exemplified by China, India and Brazil. In addition, some experts point out that the aforementioned umbrella terms may misleadingly entail a connotation of homogeneity among "new" development providers and disregard substantial differences among them. Furthermore, this divergence in views and practices is not exclusive to the so-called non-traditional donor group; in fact, established donors, too, lack homogeneity and often differ in the way they organize their aid and prioritize aid's purposes, which is evident from the multiple attempts to coordinate and harmonize their aid-giving activities and practices.

Aside from these valid criticisms, this work, however, reveals another problem associated with the established approach in the literature on international development cooperation and finds this classification problematic due to different reasons.

Indeed, "new"/Southern providers constitute as diverse and heterogeneous a group of actors as do the "Northern"/traditional donors, which appear to be held together through the process of collective identity building. In other words, "old"/"traditional"/"Northern" and "new/emerging" Southern" development actors can be conceived as members of "imagined communities", whose boundaries are shaped and reshaped through the process of "Othering". As such, providers of development cooperation, regardless of their diversity, draw lines of difference not only according to material characteristics, but through the prism of ideas, norms, values and identities that they uphold.

The first chapters described in detail the two dominant foreign aid narratives: the OECD-DAC aid and South-South development cooperation. Traditional Northern donors have established and continue to adopt the OECD-DAC assistance approach and have historically been operating under a North–South logic, which postulates that aid from "a rich and powerful North" has to be transferred to "the poor and marginalized South". So, the narratives embraced by the countries of the "Global North" emphasize charity and moral obligation toward: the less fortunate "Global South", transfer of expertise based on the Northern "superior" knowledge, and the virtues of suspending recipients' obligation to reciprocate. As it was explained in the provided discussion, in this context, the "North/South" divide should not be interpreted as denoting a geographical space, but rather must be understood metaphorically.

In contrast to this, the growing South-South Cooperation framework originates from the Bandung Conference of 1955 and promotes a vision of emancipatory, state-led development with the countries of the Global South uniting and working in solidarity against the Global North. In particular, the concept of SSC finds its roots in the struggle for independence of Asian and African countries during the 1940s and later in the Non-Aligned Movement (NAM), the idea of a common identity, equality and solidarity between less-developed countries; the defense of the sovereignty of newly independent states; and opposition to the "North" are the core elements of SSC.

Hence, the SSC narratives, embraced by the so-called Southern donors, have generally stressed principles of solidarity and equality between partners, sharing knowledge based on experience, political non-interference and the virtue of mutual benefit and recognition of reciprocity. Thus, even though SSC development assistance diverges in priorities, policies, institutional arrangements and engagement with international forums and initiatives, these providers often share a common "Southern identity", which differs from that of the Northern "Others".

As such, the Global North/Global South, developed/developing, the First World/the Third World countries lie at the core of theorization about the North-South and South-South aid paradigm. Moreover, as noted in previous chapters, the "rise of the South" in recent decades has led to fundamental shifts in global development ideas, practices, norms and actors. This book highlights that the existing literature is mainly concerned with "old"/Northern and "new"/Southern donors and argues that Kazakhstan does not fit either of these categories and in fact stands as an "outlier", falling outside any of these groups due to its historical experiences.

First, Kazakhstan was not an independent member of the global system at the time of the "First-Second-Third World" classification, and hence was not categorized as a "Third World" state when the term was first coined. Some might argue that the dissolution of the Soviet communist bloc pushed the former Soviet socialist republics from the Second World to the Third World group. While we can find economic justifications for such categorization, this transition does not make much sense according to the political criterion of the Third World. In particular, the countries of the former Soviet bloc did not join the Non-Aligned Movement upon gaining their independence in the early 1990s. Instead, they were largely interested in adopting "development-oriented" policies and practices and were eagerly learning from the experience of the First World nations at least in the first years of independence.

Thus, the re-categorization of these states, including Kazakhstan, from the Second to the Third World countries, which some defined as "re-joining the Third World", can only be justified by the fact that, as the Soviet Union ceased to exist, post-communist countries experienced a decline in the level of development. However, this observation opens up a bigger debate regarding the meaning of the word "development", considering these nations' relatively high performance in education, human capital and other development indexes, which has been discussed in detail in Chapter 5. Hence, while some labeled this transformation of the former socialist republics as their "re-joining" the Third World camp, it arguably would be more accurate to conceptualize the process as "de-development". As such, Kazakhstan, as a post-communist country, was committed to development, but not to reviving the ailing Third Worldism. This study therefore finds the practice of incorporating Kazakhstan into the new/Southern donor group, which was built on the post-colonial struggle for independence and the principles of the Non-Aligned Movement (NAM), rather problematic.

Secondly, prior to independence in 1991, Kazakhstan didn't follow the "western modernization", but was a subject of soviet modernization. Therefore, there are some serious drawbacks in theoretical assumptions and conceptual tools that scholars in development studies should be uncomfortable with when applying to post-communist context. This research argues that while development and postcolonial studies focus on the relation of the former First world/"global North" and the Third world/"global South", we know relatively little about the role and position of the former Second World countries in the development aid landscape. Postcolonial studies developed out of an entirely different range of historic and geo-historic experiences. Given the socio-political and cultural differences between Western and post-Soviet societies, we cannot assume that the methodological tools and theoretical perspectives developed in Western context are necessarily applicable to Kazakhstan.

Third, the observed phenomenon points at the general persistent invisibility of the post-Soviet space in social sciences. Despite some noticeable progress in relevant scholarship, there are still many more unanswered questions, untested theories and untranslated evidence pertaining to various phenomena observed in our underexplored region. In this book, the author demonstrates that Kazakhstan presents a challenge to the spatial matrices underpinning current postcolonial thinking, particularly the Global North/South distinction in current debate on development cooperation and the histories of colonialism.

Selected Notes and Meanings

Term	*Definition*
AUL	[Kazakh: *Auyl*] Traditional rural type settlement, camp, community among peoples of Central Asia and the Caucasus
GLAVPOLITPROSVET	[Russian: *Главполитпросвет - Главный политико-просветительный комитет Народного комиссариата просвещения*] The Main Political and Educational Committee of the People's Commissariat of Education (direct translation) was a governing body that, as the Main Directorate, was part of the People's Commissariat of Education and was engaged in political, enlightenment, as well as in agitation and propaganda work. It was established by the decree of the Council of People's Commissars on November 12, 1920. The body was engaged in the eradication of illiteracy, and was in charge of reading houses, clubs, libraries, adult schools, Soviet-party schools, communist universities, etc

(continued)

N. Insebayeva, *Modernity, Development and Decolonization of Knowledge in Central Asia*, Politics and History in Central Asia,
https://doi.org/10.1007/978-981-16-5117-5

(continued)

Term	*Definition*
GUBKOM	[Russian: *Губком - Губернский Комитет*] Guberniya (province) Committee of the Communist Party
KALYM	[Kazakh: *Qalym*] Kalym, also known as bride price, is an ancient tradition of the people of Central Asia and other regions, which was given to the bride's parents by the groom's family as a payment for bringing up their daughter
KAZRAIKOM	[Russian: *Казрайком - Казахский Районный Комитет*] Kazakh District Committee of the Communist Party
KIRPEDTECHNIKUM	[Russian: *Кирпедтехникум - Киргизский Педагогический Техникум*] Kirgiz Pedagogical Technikum (Teacher Training School)
KIRSHKOLY	[Russian: *Киршколы - Киргизские Школы*] Kirgiz (Kazakh) schools—schools where the primary language of instruction was planned to be Kazakh
KIRUCHITEL'STVO	[Russian: *Киручительство - Киргизское учительство*] Kirgiz teachers
KOMINFORMBYURO	[Russian: *Коминформбюро - Коммунистическое Информационное Бюро*] Communist Information Bureau (direct translation) or the Information Bureau of the Communist and Workers' Parties was the official central organization of the International Communist Movement (1947–1956)

(continued)

(continued)

Term	*Definition*
KORENIZATSIYA	[Russian: *Коренизация*] The policy of korenizatsiya or nativization was an early Soviet initiative designed to integrate non-Russian nationalities into the governments of their particular soviet socialist republics. Generally speaking, during the 1920s the policy was used to promote representatives of the titular nation, and national minorities, into the lower administrative-levels of the local government of their Soviet republics
KOSHCHI UNION (SOYUZ KOSHCHI)	[Russian: *Союз Кошчи*] The Koshchi Union was a mass organization (union) of working peasants in the Turkestan Autonomous Soviet Socialist Republic (and after its disengagement, in the national republics of Central Asia and Kazakhstan). Created by the decision of the 5th Congress of the Communist Party of Turkestan (September 1920) to develop existing committees and unions of poor peasants
KRASNYE YURTY	[Russian: *Красные Юрты*] The Red Yurts initiative was a campaign, which was adopted in the late 1920s to serve the nomadic and semi-nomadic female population, and was aimed at promoting literacy, health care and vocational training among those
NARKOMAT	[Russian: *Наркомат - Народный Комиссариат*] A People's Commissariat was a central government structure in the Soviet Union from 1917 to 1946. The Commissariats were analogous to the ministries and were in charge of managing specific sectors of state activity

(continued)

(continued)

Term	*Definition*
NARKOMSOVKHOZOV	[Russian: ***Наркомсовхозов - Народный комиссариат зерновых и животноводческих совхозов СССР***] The People's Commissariat of Grain and Livestock State Farms of the USSR was entrusted with planning, organizational and operational-production management of grain and livestock state farms
NARKOMZEM	[Russian: ***Наркомзем - Народный Комиссариат Земледелия***] The People's Commissariat for Agriculture, which was established in 1929, and was renamed to the Soviet Ministry of Agriculture and Food in 1946
OBKOM	[Russian: *Обком - Областной Комитет*] Oblast Committee of the Communist Party
OKRUZHKOM	[Russian: *Окружком - Окружной Комитет*] Regional Committee of the Communist Party
PROFOBR	[Russian: *Профобр - Профессиональное образование*] Professional (vocational) education
SHKOLY PERVOI STUPENI	[Russian: *Школы первой ступени*] First-level school was an elementary 5-year (since 1923 4-year) comprehensive school in the Soviet Union which was later reorganized to primary school
SHKOLY VTOROI STUPENI	[Russian: *Школы второй ступени*] Second-level school was a secondary school in the Soviet Union, which consisted of grades 6–9 (since 1923 5–9), which was later officially reorganized into secondary school
SISTEMA BRONIROVANIYA MEST	[Russian: *Система бронирования мест*] Placement reservation system was created by the Soviet regime as a system of university admission quotas
SOVKHOZ	[Russian: *Совхоз - Советское Хозяйство*] Sovkhoz was a state-owned farm in the Soviet Union
VTUZ	[Russian: *ВТУЗ - Высшее Техническое Учебное Заведение*] Higher technical education institution

(continued)

(continued)

Term	*Definition*
VUZ	[Russian: *ВУЗ - Высшее Учебное Заведение*] Higher education institution
ZHENOTDEL	[Russian: *Женотдел - Женский Отдел*] Zhenotdel is the women's department under the Central Committee and local committees devoted to the work among women. They were created in 1919 on the basis of the Agitation and Propaganda Commissions among workers and peasants
ZHENSEKTOR	[Russian: *Женсектор - Женский Сектор*] Women's Sectors were successors of local Zhenotdels

Archival Documents

Kazakhskyi kraevoi komitet RKP (b)—VKP (b) (Kazraikom RKP(b)—VKP(b)), Agitatsionno-propaganditskiy otdel, gorod Kyzyl-Orda, "Materialy o rabote agit.prop.otdela Kazaraikoma RKP (b). Dokladnye: o gramotnosti kazakhskogo naseleniya i dr. Istoricheskie spravki, protokoly agit.prop." fond 141, opis 1, ed. Kr. №336, 1925 god, na 47 listah [Kazakh Regional Committee of the Russian Communist Party (of the Bolsheviks)—All Union Communist Party (of the Bolsheviks) (Kazraikom RKP (b)—VKP (b)), Propaganda-Agitation Department, Kyzyl-Orda City, "Materials About the Work of the Propaganda-Agitation Department of Kazraikom RKP (b). Reporting: On the Literacy of the Kazakh Population and Other Historical Information, Protocols of the Propaganda-Agitation Department", fund 141, inventory 1, #336, 47 pages, 1925].

Kazakhskyi kraevoi komitet RKP (b)—VKP (b) (Kazraikom RKP(b)—VKP(b)), Agitatsionno-propaganditskiy otdel, "Protokol krayev. konferenciy po rabochemu i krestyanskomu obrazovaniyu" fond 141, opis 1, ed. Kr. №1525, 1927 god, na 506 listah [Kazakh Regional Committee of the Russian Communist Party (of the Bolsheviks) - All Union Communist Party (of the Bolsheviks) (Kazraikom RKP (b)—VKP (b)), Propaganda-Agitation Department, "Protocol of Regional Conferences on Worker and Peasant Education" fund 141, inventory 1, #1525, 506 pages, 1927.]

N. Insebayeva, *Modernity, Development and Decolonization of Knowledge in Central Asia*, Politics and History in Central Asia,
https://doi.org/10.1007/978-981-16-5117-5

Kazakhskyi kraevoi komitet RKP (b)—VKP (b) (Kazraikom RKP(b)—VKP(b)), Organizatsionno-raspredelitelnyi informats. Stat. protdel, "Obzory, spravki, svodki o sostoyanii i rabote Uralskogo Aktubinskogo i Akmolinskogo Gubkomov VKP(b) Kustanaiskogo okruzhkoma i Karakalpakskogo obkoma VKP(b) i o rabote sredi zhenshchin KSSR," fond 141, opis 1, ed. Kr. №697, 1926 god, na 165 listah [Kazakh Regional Committee of the Russian Communist Party (of the Bolsheviks)—All Union Communist Party (of the Bolsheviks) (Kazraikom RKP (b)—VKP (b)), Organization and Distribution Information Statistics Division, "Reviews, References, Reports on the Status and Work of the Ural Aktobe and Akmola Gubkoms VKP (b) of the Kostanai Okruzhkom and Karakalpak Obkom VKP (b) and on the Work Among Women in the Kazakh Soviet Socialist Republic," fund 141, inventory 1, #697, 165 pages, 1926].

Kazakhskyi kraevoi komitet RKP (b)—VKP (b) (Kazraikom RKP(b)—VKP(b)), Otdel Rabotnits i krestyan, gorod Kyzyl-Orda, "Materialy po voprosu zhenskogo obrazovaniya v Kazakhstane. Materialy o vovlechenii zhenshchin v shkoly, VUZy, Vtuzy, Komvuzy, kluby, krasnye usoiki i td. Svodki o rabote delegatskih sobraniy i dr. za 1928," fond 141, opis 1, ed. Kr. №2370, 1928 god, na 69 listah [Kazakh Regional Committee of the Russian Communist Party (of the Bolsheviks)—All Union Communist Party (of the Bolsheviks) (Kazraikom RKP (b)—VKP (b)), Propaganda-Agitation Department, Kyzyl-Orda City, "Materials on the Issue of Female Education in Kazakhstan. Materials on the Involvement of Women in Schools, University, Technical Schools, Communist Institutions of Higher Education, Clubs, etc. Delegate Meeting Summaries and Others for 1928," fund 141, inventory 1, #2370, 69 pages, 1928].

Kazakhskyi kraevoi komitet RKP (b)—VKP (b) (Kazraikom RKP(b)—VKP(b)), Otdel Rabotnits i krestyanok, "Material, tezisy, programy dlya zhen.kursov po voprosam o vozniknovenii soyuza koshchi, KSSR, po ohrane mat., zemleustroistve, zhivotnovodstve i po antireligioznoi rabote," fond 141, opis 1, ed. Hr. #1607, 1927 god, na 63 listah [Kazakh Regional Committee of the Russian Communist Party (of the Bolsheviks)—All Union Communist Party (of the Bolsheviks) (Kazraikom RKP (b)—VKP (b)), Department of Women Workers and Peasants, "Material, Theses, Programmes for Female Courses on the Emergence of the Koshchi Union, Kazakh Soviet Socialist Republic, On Mother Protection, Land Management, Animal Husbandry and Anti-religious Work," fund 141, inventory 1, #1607, 63 pages, 1927].

Tsentralnyi Komitet KP(b) Kazakhstana, gor. Alma-Ata, Otdel rukovodyashchih partiynyh organov Zhensektor, "Dokladnye zapiski i spravki obkomov i raikomov KP(b) Kazakhstana o realizatsii resheniy II syezda partii po rabote sredi zhenshchin, Spiski zhenshchin, vydvinutyh na otvetstvennye raboty" fond 708, opis 2/1, ed. Kr. №649, 1938 god, na 165 listah [The Central Committee of the Communist Party (of the Bolsheviks), Alma-Ata City, Department of the Governing Party Body of the Zhensektor, "Memos and References of the Regional and District Committees of the Communist Party (of the Bolsheviks) of Kazakhstan on the Implementation of Decisions of the II Congress of the Party for Work among Women, Lists of Women Nominated for Responsible Work", fund 708, inventory 2/1, #649, 165 pages, 1938].

Tsentraln'nyi Komitet KP(b) Kazakhstana, gor. Alma-Ata, Sel'sko-hozyaistvennyi sektor podgotovki sel'skozyaistvennyh kadrov, Ukazaniya TSKKP (b) Kazakhstana, dokladnye zapiski otdela, obkomov partii, narkomatov sovkhozov i zemledeliya Kazakhskoi SSR ob obespechenii mekhanizatorskimi kadrami i podgotovki massovoy kvalifikatsii dlya sel'skogo hozyaistva, fund 708, opis' 411, №1217, na 78 listah, 1940—"Svodnaya ot 1939 goda [The Central Committee of the Communist Party (of the Bolsheviks), Alma-Ata City, Agricultural Sector for Training of Agricultural Cadres, A Decree by the Central Committee of the Communist Party (b) of Kazakhstan, Department Memos, Province Party Committee Memos, Memos of A People's Commissariat for the State Farms and Agriculture of the Kazakh Soviet Socialist Republic About Providing Mechanization Personnel and Preparing Mass Qualifications for the Rural Economy, fund 708, inventory 411, #1217, 78 pages, 1940].

Bibliography

Abdurasulov, A. (2016, May 23). Razgon protestov v Kazakhstane: rasskazy ochevidcev. *BBC*. http://www.bbc.com/russian/international/2016/05/160523_kazakhstan_protests

Acharya, A., & Buzan, B. (2010). *Non-Western international relations theory: Perspectives on and beyond Asia* (1st ed.). Routledge.

ADB $1 Billion loan to help Kazakhstan counter economic slowdown. (2015). Retrieved from Asian Development Bank website https://www.adb.org/news/adb-1-billion-loan-help-kazakhstan-counter-economic-slowdown

Aid at a glance charts. (2015). *Organization for Economic Cooperation and Development*. http://www.oecd.org/countries/kazakhstan/aid-at-a-glance.htm

Aitmukhambetov, A., & Ardabayeva, F. (2014). Vneshnyaia politika Kazakhstana i Organizaciya Ob'yedinennykh Natcii sovremennogo Kazakhstana. In *Baitursynovskie tchteniya* (pp. 59–63). Kostanai.

Anderson, B. (1983). *Imagined Communities* (1st ed.). Verso.

Andrzejczak, K., & Kliber, A. (2016). Development cooperation with African countries: Models based on donor approach and recipient structure. In C. Talesco, F. Sai Kit Ng, & D. Ip (Eds.), *Development: What now? Past, present and future. Challenges in international development* (pp. 292–322). PolyU.

Aneja, U. (2018). South-South cooperation and competition. In E. Fiddian-Qasmiyeh & P. Daley (Eds.), *Routledge handbook of South-South relations* (1st ed., pp. 141–152). Routledge.

Arase, D. (Ed.). (2005). *Japan's foreign aid: Old continuities and new directions*. Routledge.

N. Insebayeva, *Modernity, Development and Decolonization of Knowledge in Central Asia*, Politics and History in Central Asia,
https://doi.org/10.1007/978-981-16-5117-5

Baigarin, M. (2014, October 29). Mazhilis odobril proekt, sistematiziruyushy pomosh razvitiyu drugih stran. *Kazinform*. http://www.inform.kz:8080/rus/article/2711069

Baimanov, D. (2017, March 13). Mazhilismen obyasnil pomosh Kazakhstana drugim stranam. *Kazinform*. http://www.kazinform.kz/ru/mazhilismen-ob-yasnil-pomosch-kazahstana-drugim-stranam_a3007294

Bendini, R. (2013). *Kazakhstan: Selected trade and economic issues* (Policy briefing). http://www.europarl.europa.eu/RegData/etudes/briefing_note/join/2013/522303/EXPO-INTA_SP(2013)522303_EN.pdf

Bergamaschi, I., Moore, P., & Tickner, A. (2017). *South-South cooperation beyond the myths. Rising donors, new aid practices?* (1st ed.). Palgrave Macmillan.

Berger, M. (1948). How the Molotov Plan works. *The Antioch Review, 8*(1), 17–25.

Berger, M. (1994). The end of the 'Third World'? *Third World Quarterly, 15*(2), 257–275. Retrieved March 14, 2020, from www.jstor.org/stable/3993146

Busan Partnership agreement. (2012). https://www.oecd.org/dac/effectiveness/Busan%20partnership.pdf

Campbell, E. I. (2015). *The Muslim question and Russian imperial governance*. Indiana University Press.

Clark, H. (2015, May 21). *Speech at the Astana Economic Forum on "Africa: The next driver of the global economy"*. http://www.undp.org/content/undp/en/home/presscenter/speeches/2015/05/21/helen-clark-speech-at-the-astana-economic-forum-on-africa-the-next-driver-of-the-global-economy-.html

Chandy, L. (2012). New in Town: A look at the role of emerging donors in an evolving aid system. *Brookings*. https://www.brookings.edu/articles/new-in-town-a-look-at-the-role-of-emerging-donors-in-an-evolving-aid-system/

Chin, G., & Quadir, F. (2012). Introduction: Rising states, rising donors and the global aid regime. *Cambridge Review of International Affairs, 25*(4), 493–506.

Concept of the Republic of Kazakhstan in the sphere of official development assistance. (2013). *Government of the Republic of Kazakhstan*. https://tengrinews.kz/zakon/pravitelstvo_respubliki_kazahstan_premer_ministr_rk/konstitutsionnyiy_stroy_i_osnovyi_gosudarstvennogo_upravleniya/id-P1300000240/

Consolidated version of the Treaty on European Union. Chapter 1: General provisions on the Union's external action—Article 21. (2008). http://eur-lex.europa.eu/legal-content/EN/TXT/?uri=CELEX%3A12008M021

Corruption Perception Index: Kazakhstan. (2016). *Transparency International*. https://www.transparency.org/country/KAZ

DAC List of ODA recipients. (2016). https://www.oecd.org/dac/stats/documentupload/DAC%20List%20of%20ODA%20Recipients%202014%20final.pdf

Darwin, J. (1988). *Britain and decolonisation: The retreat from empire in the post-war world*. Macmillan.

De Cordier, B. (2014). Kazakhstan and Azerbaijan as donors of humanitarian aid: Has the diversification of aid channels and donors reached Southern Eurasia? *Central Asia and the Caucasus, 15*(4).

De la Croix, D., & Delavallade, C. (2013). Why corrupt governments may receive more foreign aid? *Oxford Economic Papers, 66*(1), 51–66. https://academic.oup.com/oep/article/66/1/51/2362604/Why-corrupt-governments-may-receive-more-foreign

Democratic Party Ak Zhol. (2014, September 9). Predlozheniya chlenov deputatskoy frakcii DPK Ak Zhol k proektu Zakona Respubliki Kazakhstan "Ob oficialnoy pomoshi razvitiyu".

Division of labor among donors—An approach to harmonization. (2010, February). *Input paper for the evaluation of the Paris Declaration (Phase 2)*. https://www.oecd.org/dac/evaluation/dcdndep/44729615.pdf

Dlya chego Kazakhstan sozdal regional'nuyu systemu pomoshi razvitiyu KazAID. (2015, September 27). *UN Radio*. http://www.unmultimedia.org/radio/russian/archives/201932/#.WOhRaPmGPIV

Donald, G. (1983). *U.S. foreign aid and the national interest*. National Planning Association

Dubuisson, E. (2017). *Reflections on a workshop "The future of Central Asian studies"*. [Blog] http://thecessblog.com/2017/10/reflections-on-a-workshop-the-future-of-central-asian-studies/

Dzhakupov, K. (2015, July 15). *Speech at the closing of the fourth Parliaments session of the Vth convocation*. http://www.parlam.kz/ru/mazhilis/news-details/id24660/1/1

Engel, S. (2019). South-South Cooperation in Southeast Asia: From Bandung and Solidarity to Norms and Rivalry. *Journal of Current Southeast Asian Affairs, 38*(2), 218–242.

Escobar, A. (1995). *Encountering development: The making and unmaking of the Third World* (1st ed.). Princeton University Press.

EU development aid. (2015). Retrieved from the Official Website of the European Union https://europa.eu/eyd2015/en/content/eu-development-aid

Eyben, R., & Savage, L. (2012). Emerging and submerging powers: Imagined geographies in the new development partnership at the Busan Fourth High Level Forum. *Journal of Development Studies, 49*(4), 457–469.

Fejerskov, A., Lundsgaarde, E., & Cold-Ravnkilde, S. (2016). Uncovering the dynamics of interaction in development cooperation: A review of the "new actors in development" research agenda. *DIIS Working Papers, 1*, 1–24.

Fiddian-Qasmiyeh, E., & Daley, P. (2018). *Routledge handbook of South-South relations* (1st ed.). Routledge.

Foreign Policy Concept for 2014–2020 of the Republic of Kazakhstan. (2014). http://mfa.gov.kz/index.php/en/component/content/article/16-materials-english/1248-foreign-policy-concept-for-2014-2020-republic-of-kazakhstan

Freedom House. (2017, January 31). *Freedom in the World 2017: Freedom decline continues amid rising populism and autocracy*. https://freedomhouse.org/article/freedom-world-2017-freedom-decline-continues-amid-rising-populism-and-autocracy

GDP (current US$): Kazakhstan. (2019). Available from the World Bank national accounts data http://data.worldbank.org/indicator/NY.GDP.MKTP.CD?locations=KZ

GDP growth (annual %): Kazakhstan. (2019). Available from the World Bank national accounts data http://data.worldbank.org/indicator/NY.GDP.MKTP.KD.ZG?locations=KZ

GHA Report 2010. (2010). *Global Humanitarian Assistance*. http://www.globalhumanitarianassistance.org/wp-content/uploads/2010/07/GHA_Report8.pdf

GHA Report 2012. (2012). *Global Humanitarian Assistance*. http://www.globalhumanitarianassistance.org/wp-content/uploads/2012/07/GHA_Report_2012-Websingle.pdf

Global Humanitarian Assistance Report 2016. (2016). *Global Humanitarian Assistance*. http://www.globalhumanitarianassistance.org/wp-content/uploads/2016/07/GHA-report-2016-full-report.pdf

Gulrajani, N., & Swiss, L. (2017). *Why do countries become donors? Assessing the drivers and implications of donor proliferation*. https://www.odi.org/sites/odi.org.uk/files/resource-documents/11364.pdf

Gulrajani, N., & Swiss, L. (2018). Donor proliferation to what ends? New donor countries and the search for legitimacy. *Canadian Journal of Development Studies / Revue canadienne d'études du développement*.

Hattori, T. (2001). Re-conceptualizing foreign aid. *Review of International Political Economy, 8*(4), 633–660. https://doi.org/10.1080/09692290110077610

History of DAC Lists of aid recipient countries. (n.d.). http://www.oecd.org/dac/stats/historyofdaclistsofaidrecipientcountries.htm

History of the 0.7% ODA target. (2002). *DAC Journal, 3*(4), 9–11. http://www.oecd.org/dac/stats/ODA-history-of-the-0-7-target.pdf

Hook, S. W. (1995). *National interest and foreign aid*. Lynne Rienner.

Insebayeva, S. (2016). *Imagining the nation: Identity, nation-building and foreign policy in Kazakhstan* (CAP Papers 175). Retrieved from Central Asia Program website http://centralasiaprogram.org/blog/2016/10/04/imagining-the-nation-identity-nation-building-and-foreign-policy-in-kazakhstan/

Is it ODA? (2008). *OECD Factsheet*. http://www.oecd.org/dac/stats/34086975.pdf

Jaffrelot, Ch. (2009). *Emerging states: The wellspring of a new world order*. Columbia University Press.

James, L., & Leake, E. (2015). *Decolonization and the Cold War* (1st ed.). Bloomsbury Academic.

Jha, M. (2016, December 2). India's connect Central Asia policy. *The Diplomat*. http://thediplomat.com/2016/12/indias-connect-central-asia-policy-2/

Kamalova, G. (2015, July 14). Kazakhstan in 10 world's worst performers in economy: Bloomberg. *Tengrinews*. https://en.tengrinews.kz/finance/Kazakhstan-in-10-Worlds-Worst-Performers-in-Economy-261070/

Kapparov, K. (2016). *Invisible pubic debt: The case of Kazakhstan* (CAP Papers 171). Retrieved from Central Asia Program website http://centralasiaprogram.org/blog/2016/07/19/the-invisible-public-debt-the-case-of-kazakhstan/

Kapoor, I. (2008). *The Postcolonial politics of development* (1st ed.). Routledge.

KazAid is key to Kazakh regional development, says Deputy FM. (2014, October 10). *Ministry of Foreign Affairs of the Republic of Kazakhstan*. http://www.mfa.kz/index.php/ru/contrast/12-material-orys/2065-astana-calling-375-1

Kazakhstan discusses further aid to Syria with Russia, Red Cross, UN. (2016, October 11). *Sputnik*. https://sputniknews.com/middleeast/201610111046229132-kazakhstan-syria-russia-un/

Kazakhstan hochet izbavitsya ot statusa poluchatelya bezvozmezdnoi pomoshi ADB. (2013, October 24). *Tengrinews*. https://tengrinews.kz/kazakhstan_news/kazahstan-hochet-izbavitsya-statusa-poluchatelya-244166/

Kazakhstan increases contributions to international organizations. (2015, January 1). *KZNewsline*. http://kznewsline.com/kazakhstan-increases-contributions-to-international-organizations/

Kazakhstan investiroval v obuchenie studentov iz Afghanistana $50 milionov. (2014, March 31). *Afghanskoe Telegraphnoe Agenstvo*. http://www.aftag.info/news-of-the-day/detail.php?ID=8614&VOTE_ID=2&view_result=Y%20http://afghanistantoday.ru/node/39876

Kazakhstan launches project on Official development assistance for Afghanistan—Ministry of Foreign Affairs of Kazakhstan. (2016). *Kazinform*. http://www.government.kz/en/novosti/1003433-kazakhstan-launches-project-on-official-development-assistance-for-afghanistan-ministry-of-foreign-affairs-of-kazakhstan.html

Kazakhstan nameren aktivizitovat rabotu v kachestve strany – donora v ramkah Aziatskogo banka razvitiya. (2014, April 22). Retrieved from the Official website of the Ministry of National Economy of the Republic of Kazakhstan http://economy.gov.kz/ru/news/detail.php?ELEMENT_ID=56863

Kazakhstan—Official Development Assistance. (2013). *Organization for Economic Cooperation and Development*. http://www.aidflows.org/KZ_Beneficiary_View.pdf

Kazakhstan okazal gumanitarnuyu pomosh 50-ti stranam mira. (2016, December 12). *Pervy Kanal Kazakhstan*.

Kazakhstan peredal gumanitarnuyu pomosh Syrii. (2017, January 6). *Tengrinews.kz*. https://tengrinews.kz/kazakhstan_news/kazahstan-peredal-gumanitarnuyu-pomosch-sirii-309564/

Kazakhstan podelilsya opytom so specialistami iz afrikanskogo kontinenta. (2015, August 4). *UNDP*. https://www.kz.undp.org/.

Kazakhstan prodolzhit pomogat Afghanistanu. (2010, December 3). *Tengrinews*. https://tengrinews.kz/osce/kazahstan-prodoljit-pomogat-afganistanu-92550/

Kazakhstan provided KZT 10 bln humanitarian aid to foreign nations. (2017, March 13). *Kazinform*. http://www.inform.kz/en/kazakhstan-provided-kzt-10-bln-humanitarian-aid-to-foreign-nations_a3007325

Kazakhstan provides humanitarian aid to Syria. (2017, January 6). *Ministry of Foreign Affairs of Republic of Kazakhstan*. http://mfa.gov.kz/index.php/en/last-news/8063-kazakhstan-provideshumanitarian-aid-to-syria

Kazakhstan ratifies loan agreement with IBRD. (2016). *Kazinform*. http://www.inform.kz/en/kazakhstan-ratifies-loan-agreement-with-ibrd_a2867794

Kazakhstan to render aid to hungry people of Somalia. (2011, August 9), *Tengrinews.kz*. https://en.tengrinews.kz/politics_sub/Kazakhstan-to-render-aid-to-hungry-people-of-Somalia-3718/

Kazakhstan secures seat on UN Security Council. (2016, June 29). *Eurasianet*. http://www.eurasianet.org/node/79446

Kazakhstan's UN bid. (2017). http://www.kazakhstanunsc.com/kazakhstans-un-bid/

Kazakhstan. (n.d.). *United Nations for the Coordination of Humanitarian Affairs—Regional Office for the Caucasus and Central Asia*. http://www.unocha.org/rocca/country-profile/kazakhstan

Kim, S., & Lightfoot, S. (2011). Does "DAC-ability" really matter? The emergence of non-DAC donors: Introduction to policy arena. *Journal of International Development, 23*, 711–721. https://doi.org/10.1002/jid.1795

Kragelund, P. (2015). Towards convergence and cooperation in the global development finance regime: Closing Africa's policy space. *Cambridge Review of International Affairs, 28*(2), 246–262.

Kragelund, P. (2019). *South-South Development* (1st ed.). Routledge.

Lancaster, C. (2007). *Foreign aid: Diplomacy, development, domestic politics*. University of Chicago Press.

Lancaster, C. (2009). Sixty years of foreign aid: What have we learned? *International Journal, 64*(3). New Perspectives on Canadian Security Studies (Summer, 2009), pp. 799–810.

Laruelle, M. (2015, May 1). The power of soft power in Kazakhstan. *The Washington Post*. https://www.washingtonpost.com/news/monkey-cage/

wp/2015/05/01/the-power-of-soft-power-in-kazakhstan/?utm_term=.a8846f59eca5

Lauria, V., & Fumagalli, C. (2019). BRICS, the southern model, and the evolving landscape of development assistance: Toward a new taxonomy. *Public Administration and Development, 39*(4–5), 215–230.

Law on Official Development Assistance. (2014). http://akzhol.kz/uploads/%D0%B7%D0%B0%D0%BA%D0%BE%D0%BD%D0%A0%D0%9A%20%D1%80%D1%83%D1%81%D1%81.pdf

Ma, S. (1998). Third World studies, development studies and post-communist studies: Definitions, distance and dynamism. *Third World Quarterly, 19*(3), 339–356.

Macekura, S. (2013). The Point Four Program and U.S. international development policy. *Political Science Quarterly, 128*(1), 127–160. www.jstor.org/stable/23563372

Malyshev, D., & Bainazarova, E. (2016). Russia and Kazakhstan: Mutually different interests for regional leadership. In H. Rytövuori-Apunen (Ed.), *The regional security puzzle around Afghanistan: Bordering practices in Central Asia and beyond* (pp. 243–270). Barbara Budrich Publishers.

Manning, R. (2006). Will "emerging donors" change the face of international cooperation? *Development Policy Review, 24*(4), 371–385. http://www.oecd.org/dac/36417541.pdf

Mawdsley, E. (2012). *From recipients to donors: Emerging powers and the changing development landscape* (1st ed.). Zed Books.

Mawdsley, E. (2015). Development geography 1. Cooperation, competition and convergence between 'North' and 'South'. *Progress in Human Geography, 41*(1), 108–117.

Mawdsley, E. (2018). Southern leaders, Northern followers? Who has 'socialized' whom in international development?. In E. Fiddian-Qasmiyeh & P. Daley, *Routledge handbook of South-South relations* (1st ed.). Routledge.

Mawdsley, E., Fourie, E., & Nauta, W. (2019). *Researching South-South development cooperation* (1st ed.). Routledge.

Mazhilismeny prinyali zakon ob oficialnoy pomoshi razvitiyu. (2014, November 26). *Today.kz.* http://today.kz/news/kazahstan/2014-11-26/591233-mazhilismeny-prinyali-zakon-ob-oficialnoj-pomoshhi-razvitiyu/

McKinlay, R. D., & Mughan, A. (1984). *Aid and arms to the third world: An analysis of the distribution and import of US official transfer*. St. Martin's.

Milner, H., & Tingley, D. H. (2013). Introduction to geopolitics of foreign aid. In *Geopolitics of Foreign Aid*. Edward Elgar.

Mirzayan, G. (2014). Kazakhstan formiruet poyas dobrososedstva. *Expert*. http://expert.ru/2014/11/13/kazahstan-formiruet-poyas-dobrososedstva/

Morgenthau, H. (1962). A political theory of foreign aid. *American Political Science Review, 56*(2), 301–309.

Mosley, P. (1987). *Foreign aid: Its defense and reform.* University Press of Kentucky.
Muller, C. (2017, January 19). World Bank: Kazakhstan achieved significant progress. *KazakhTV.* http://kazakh-tv.kz/en/view/news_kazakhstan/page_180249_
Nazarbayev, N. (2000, October 16). *Address of the President of the Republic of Kazakhstan, Nursultan Nazarbayev, to the People of Kazakhstan.* http://www.akorda.kz/ru/addresses/addresses_of_president/poslanie-prezidenta-respubliki-kazakhstan-n-a-nazarbaeva-narodu-kazakhstana-oktyabr-2000-g_1342416665
Nazarbayev, N. (2007, February 28). *Address of the President of the Republic of Kazakhstan, Nursultan Nazarbayev, to the People of Kazakhstan.* http://www.akorda.kz/ru/addresses/addresses_of_president/poslanie-prezidenta-respubliki-kazahstan-nnazarbaeva-narodu-kazahstana-28-fevralya-2007-g
Nazarbayev, N. (2010, November 2). Nursultan Nazarbayev: V nashei druzhbe net nikakih sekretov with Vasilyev, A./ Interviewer. *Rossiyskaya Gazeta.* https://rg.ru/2010/11/02/nazarbaev.html
Nazarbayev, N. (2011, January 28). *Address of the President of the Republic of Kazakhstan, Nursultan Nazarbayev, to the People of Kazakhstan.* http://www.akorda.kz/en/addresses/addresses_of_president/address-of-the-president-of-the-republic-of-kazakhstan-nursultan-nazarbayev-to-the-people-of-kazakhstan-january-28-2011_1341926571
Nazarbayev, N. (2013, April 26). *President Nazarbayev's Speech at the Almaty Ministerial Conference of the Istanbul Process on Afghanistan.* http://www.akorda.kz/ru/special/speeches/external_political_affairs/ext_speeches_and_addresses/vystuplenie-prezidenta-kazahstana-nanazarbaeva-na-konferencii-ministrov-inostrannyh-del-stran-uchastnic-stambulskogo-processa
Nazarbayev posovetoval Kyrgyzstancam bolshe rabotat. (2012, August 22). *Tengrinews.* https://tengrinews.kz/kazakhstan_news/nazarbaev-posovetoval-kyirgyizstantsam-bolshe-rabotat-219158/
Ndlovu-Gatsheni, S., & Tafira, K. (2018). The invention of the global South and the politics of South-South solidarity. In E. Fiddian-Qasmiyeh & P. Daley, *Routledge handbook of South-South relations* (1st ed.). Routledge.
Net ODA received (% of GNI): Kazakhstan. (2016). Available from the World Bank national accounts data http://data.worldbank.org/indicator/DT.ODA.ODAT.GN.ZS?locations=KZ
Noguchi, M. (2005). Globalism and developmentalism. In C. Lapavitsas & M. Noguchi, *Beyond market-driven development* (1st ed.). Routledge.
OCHA Annual Report 2015. (2016). *United Nations Office for Coordination of Humanitarian Affairs.* http://www.unocha.org/2015annualreport/2015annualreport.pdf

OCHA. (2013). *Regionalniy obzor gumanitarnogo finansirovania—Kavkaz i Tsentral'naia Azia* (No. 8 and No. 9). http://reliefweb.int/sites/reliefweb.int/files/resources/Funding%20update%20-%20second%20quarter%202013%20-%20Russian%20-%20final.pdf

ODA key statistics: Kazakhstan. (2016). http://www.oecd-ilibrary.org/development/development-co-operation-report-2016/oda-key-statistics-kazakhstan_dcr-2016-graph351-en

Official Development Assistance. (2016) *Issue Brief Series*. http://www.un.org/esa/ffd/wp-content/uploads/2016/01/ODA_OECD-FfDO_IATF-Issue-Brief.pdf

Official development assistance—Definition and coverage. (n.d.). http://www.oecd.org/dac/stats/officialdevelopmentassistancedefinitionandcoverage.htm#Definition

Opening Statement by H.E. Erlan Idrissov, Former Minister of Foreign Affairs of the Republic of Kazakhstan, at the VIII Astana Economic Forum "Africa—The World's Next Economic Driver". (2015, May 21). *Ministry of Foreign Affairs of Republic of Kazakhstan*. http://www.mfa.gov.kz/index.php/en/last-news/3916-opening-statement-by-h-e-erlan-idrissov-minister-of-foreign-affairs-of-the-republic-of-kazakhstan-at-the-viii-astana-economic-forum-africa-the-world-s-next-economic-driver

Orazgaliyeva, M. (2014, October 31). Kazakhstan's Official Development Assistance to focus on Central Asia, Afghanistan, says FM. *Astana Times*. http://astanatimes.com/2014/10/kazakhstans-official-development-assistance-focus-central-asia-afghanistan-says-fm/

Orazgaliyeva, M. (2015, May 18). Astana Economic Forum to feature sessions on Africa, KazAID. *Astana Times*. http://astanatimes.com/2015/05/astana-economic-forum-to-feature-sessions-on-africa-kazaid/

Orazgaliyeva, M. (2015, May 26). Kazakhstan to provide $200,000 in humanitarian aid to Nepal. *Astana Times*. http://astanatimes.com/2015/05/kazakhstan-to-provide-200000-in-humanitarian-aid-to-nepal/

Orazgaliyeva, M. (2017, April 26). Central Asian farmers trained in latest agro-technologies as part of Kazakhstan's development assistance. *Astana Times*. http://astanatimes.com/2017/04/central-asian-farmers-trained-in-latest-agro-technologies-as-part-of-kazakhstans-development-assistance/

Organization for Economic Cooperation and Development (OECD). (2016a). *Aid (ODA) disbursements to countries and regions*. http://stats.oecd.org/Index.aspx?DataSetCode=Table2A

Organization for Economic Cooperation and Development (OECD). (2016b). *Development Co-operation Report 2016: The sustainable development goals as business opportunities*. OECD Publishing.

Organization for Economic Cooperation and Development (OECD). (2016c). *Multi-dimensional review of Kazakhstan: Volume 1. Initial assessment*. OECD Publishing

Organization for Economic Cooperation and Development (OECD). (2017). *Development finance of countries beyond the DAC*. http://www.oecd.org/development/stats/non-dac-reporting.htm

Palmer, G., Wohlander, S. B., & Morgan, T. C. (2002). Give or take: Foreign aid and foreign policy substitutability. *Journal of Peace Research, 39*(1), 5–26. http://www.jstor.org/stable/425255

Pannier, B. (2016, May 22). The reasons Kazakhs are protesting. *Radio Liberty*. https://www.rferl.org/a/qishloq-ovozi-kazakhstan-reasons-behind-protests/27750185.html

Pieterse, J. N. (1991). Dilemmas of development discourse: The crisis of developmentalism and the comparative method. *Development and Change, 22*(1), 5–29. https://doi.org/10.1111/j.1467-7660.1991.tb00401.x

Pomfret, R. (2005). Kazakhstan's economy since independence: Does the oil boom offer a second chance for sustainable development? *Europe-Asia Studies, 57*(6), 859–876. https://www.jstor.org/stable/30043927?seq=1#page_scan_tab_contents

Posega, P. (2015). Kazakhstan beyond Borat. *Modern Diplomacy*. http://moderndiplomacy.eu/index.php?option=com_k2&view=item&id=763:kazakhstan-beyond-borat&Itemid=772

Premature donors? Development aid from Central and Eastern Europe ten years on. (2013, November 28). https://blogs.ucl.ac.uk/ssees/2013/11/28/premature-donors-development-aid-from-central-and-eastern-europe-ten-years-on/

Putz, C. (2015, December 22). Central Asia 'extremely important' to the European Union. *The Diplomat*. http://thediplomat.com/2015/12/central-asia-extremely-important-to-the-european-union/

Radcliffe, S. A. (2005). Development and geography: Towards a postcolonial development geography? *Progress in Human Geography, 29*(3), 291–298. https://doi.org/10.1191/0309132505ph548pr

Raghuram, P., Noxolo, P., & Madge, C. (2013). Rising Asia and postcolonial geography. *Singapore Journal of Tropical Geography, 35*(1), 119–135. https://doi.org/10.1111/sjtg.12045

Rapley, J. (2004). Development studies and the post-development critique. *Progress in Development Studies, 4*(4), 350–354. https://doi.org/10.1191/1464993404ps095pr

Regional Development Cooperation Strategy 2015–2019. (2014). *USAID: Central Asia*. http://pdf.usaid.gov/pdf_docs/PBAAB464.pdf

Renzio, P., & Seifert, J. (2014). South-South cooperation and the future of development assistance: Mapping actors and options. *Third World Quarterly, 35*(10), 1860–1875.

Roberts, G. (1994). Moscow and the Marshall plan: Politics, ideology and the onset of the Cold War, 1947. *Europe-Asia Studies, 46*(8), 1371–1386. http://www.jstor.org/stable/152768

Rosser, A., & Tubilewicz, C. (2016). Emerging donors and new contests over aid policy in Pacific Asia. *The Pacific Review, 29*(1), 5–19. https://doi.org/10.1080/09512748.2015.1066413

Rowlands, D. (2008). *Emerging donors in international development assistance: A synthesis report.* https://www.idrc.ca/sites/default/files/sp/Documents%20EN/donors-international-development-synthesis-report.pdf

Rowlands, D. (2012). Individual BRICS or a collective bloc? Convergence and divergence amongst 'emerging donor' nations. *Cambridge Review of International Affairs, 25*(4), 629–649.

Ryan, H. (1993). President Harry S. Truman's inaugural address. In H. Ryan, *The inaugural addresses of twentieth-century American presidents* (1st ed., pp.141–152). Praeger Publishers.

Sachs, W. (1992). *The development dictionary: A guide to knowledge as power* (1st ed.). Zed Books.

Sato, J., Shiga, H., Kobayashi, T., & Kondoh, H. (2010). *How do "emerging" donors differ from "traditional" donors? An institutional analysis of foreign aid.* Retrieved from JICA-RI Website https://www.jica.go.jp/jica-ri/publication/workingpaper/jrft3q00000022dd-att/JICA-RI_WP_No.2_2010.pdf

Scott, J., vom Hau, M., & Hulme, D. (2010). *Beyond the BRICS: Identifying the "emerging middle powers" and understanding their role in global poverty reduction* (Working Paper, BWPI, 137).

Seifert, J. (2016). New dynamics or old patterns? South-South Cooperation between Brazil and Angola. In J. van der Merwe, I. Taylor, & A. Arkhangelskaya (Eds.), *Emerging powers in Africa: A new wave in the relationship?* (1st ed., pp. 129–157). Palgrave Macmillan.

Seisembayeva, A. (2017, January 9). Kazakhstan provides additional humanitarian aid to Syria. *Astana Times.* http://astanatimes.com/2017/01/kazakhstan-provides-additional-humanitarian-aid-to-syria/

Senat vernul v Mazhilis zakonoproekt ob oficialnoy pomoshi razvitiyu. (2014, November 20). *Today.kz.* http://meta.kz/novosti/kazakhstan/940426-senat-vernul-v-mazhilis-zakonoproekt-ob-oficialnoy-pomoschi-razvitiyu.html

Shimomura, Y., & Ping, W. (2015). *Chains of knowledge creation and emerging donors* (JICA-RI Working Papers 88). https://www.jica.go.jp/jica-ri/publication/workingpaper/jrft3q000000262n-att/JICA-RI_WP_No.88.pdf

Simon, D. (2006). Separated by common ground? Bringing (post)development and (post)colonialism together. *The Geographical Journal, 172*(1), 10–21. Retrieved March 6, 2020, from www.jstor.org/stable/4134870

SlovakAid. (2017). http://www.slovakaid.sk/en/slovakaid

Sylvester, C. (1999). Development studies and postcolonial studies: Disparate tales of the "Third World." *Third World Quarterly, 20*(4), 703–721. https://doi.org/10.1080/01436599913514

Technical Guide to terms and data in the Creditor Reporting System (CRS) Aid Activities database. (n.d.). http://www.oecd.org/dac/stats/crsguide.htm

The DAC: 50 years, 50 highlights. (2010). http://www.oecd.org/dac/46717535.pdf

Trading Economics. (2016). *Kazakhstan Gross External Debt 1995–2017*. http://www.tradingeconomics.com/kazakhstan/external-debt

Truman, H. (1949). *Inaugural address of Harry S. Truman Speech*. The Avalon Project. Documents in Law, History and Diplomacy. https://avalon.law.yale.edu/20th_century/truman.asp

Tull, S. (2014, July 14). Kazakhstan, UNDP work on developing country's aid agency with Mager, Y./Interviewer. *Astana Times*. http://astanatimes.com/2014/07/kazakhstan-un-work-developing-countrys-aid-agency/

Turebekova, A. (2015, June 26). Czech development cooperation experience could be useful for KazAID. *Astana Times*. http://astanatimes.com/2015/06/czech-development-cooperation-experience-could-be-useful-for-kazaid/

Turebekova, A. (2015, July 5). German Society for Int'l Cooperation shares development assistance experience. *Astana Times*. http://astanatimes.com/2015/07/german-society-for-intl-cooperation-shares-development-assistance-experience/

Turebekova, A. (2015, October 6). Kazakhstan, UNDP to assist African countries with sustainable development goals. *Astana Times*. http://astanatimes.com/2015/10/kazakhstan-undp-to-assist-african-countries-with-sustainable-development-goals/

Qian, N. (2014). *Making progress on foreign aid* (Annual Review of Economics 3). http://aida.wss.yale.edu/~nq3/NANCYS_Yale_Website/resources/papers/Aid_20140816_FINAL.pdf

Quinn, B. (2017, January 4). UK among six countries to hit 0.7% UN aid spending target. *The Guardian*. https://www.theguardian.com/global-development/2017/jan/04/uk-among-six-countries-hit-un-aid-spending-target-oecd

Ukaz 415: Ob utverzhdenii osnovnyh napravleny gosudarstvennoi politiki Respubliki Kazakhstan v sfere oficialnoy pomoshi razvitiyu na 2017–2020 gody. (2014). http://egov.kz/cms/ru/law/list/U1700000415

UN. (2007, November 13). *Kazakhstan budet dobivatsya izbraniya v sostav Soveta Bezopasnosti.* http://www.un.org/russian/news/story.asp?newsID=8600#.WUoZx-uGPIV

UN. (2010). *Security Council Elections 2010* (Special research report No. 3). http://www.securitycouncilreport.org/special-research-report/lookup-c-glKWLeMTIsG-b-6238577.php?print=true

UNDP. (2017). *AFRICANA project brief*. www.kz.undp.org/content/dam/kazakhstan/AFRICANA_project_brief_ENG.doc

UNESCO. (2012). *Education for all global monitoring report 2012.* http://www.unesco.org/fileadmin/MULTIMEDIA/HQ/ED/pdf/gmr2012-report-edi.pdf

Wallace, P. (2016, August 23). World's worst currency slump gleaning rewards for Nigeria. *Bloomberg.* https://www.bloomberg.com/news/articles/2016-08-23/world-s-worst-currency-slump-starts-to-glean-rewards-for-nigeria

Vstrechaem gostei iz Afriki! (2015, October 22). *Zhasatyrau.* http://zhasatyrau.kz/news/apec.html

Walker, J., & Kearney, K. (2016, September 16). What Central Asia means to the United States. *The Diplomat.* http://thediplomat.com/2016/09/what-central-asia-means-to-the-united-states/

Walz, J., & Ramachandran, V. (2011). *Brave new world: A literature review of emerging donors and the changing nature of foreign assistance* (Center for Global Development Working Paper 273). https://www.cgdev.org/publication/brave-new-world-literature-review-emerging-donors-and-changing-nature-foreign-assistance

Wendt, A. (1992). Anarchy is what states make of it: The social construction of power politics. *International Organization, 46*(2), 391–425. https://www.jstor.org/stable/2706858?seq=1#page_scan_tab_contents

Wendt, A. (1999). *Social theory of international politics.* Cambridge University Press.

White, J. (1974). *The politics of foreign aid.* Bodley Head.

Williams, G., Meth, P., & Willis, K. (2009). *Geographies of developing areas: The global south in a changing world* (1st ed.). Routledge.

Wissenbach, U. (2010). A new Seoul consensus on development: The G20 needs to reconcile effective ODA with emerging country economic cooperation. In T. Fues & P. Wolff, *G20 and Global Development: How can the new summit architecture promote pro-poor growth and sustainability?* (1st ed., pp. 26–29). German Development Institute.

Witte, M. (2015, May 26). ICRC seeks increased dialogue with Kazakhstan on KazAID, Humanitarian work. *Astana Times.* http://astanatimes.com/2015/05/icrc-seeks-increased-dialogue-with-kazakhstan-on-kazaid-humanitarian-work/

Witter, M. (2015, May 27). UNDP seeks stronger Kazakh partnership, says country key to South-South Cooperation. *Astana Times*. http://astanatimes.com/2015/05/undp-seeks-stronger-kazakh-partnership-says-country-key-to-south-south-cooperation/

Woods, N. (2008). Whose aid? Whose influence? China, emerging donors and the silent revolution in development assistance. *International Affairs, 84*(6), 1205–1221. http://nghiencuuquocte.net/wp-content/uploads/2014/02/China-emerging-donors-and-the-silent-revolution-in-development-assistance.pdf

World Bank—Kazakhstan partnership program snapshot. (2016). Available from the World Bank website http://pubdocs.worldbank.org/en/220651460698981308/Kazakhstan-Snapshot-s2016-en.pdf

World Bank to help Kazakhstan SMEs become more competitive. (2015). Available from the World Bank website http://www.worldbank.org/en/news/press-release/2015/03/02/world-bank-kazakhstan-smes-competitive

Yamada, S. (2016). *Post-education-for-all and sustainable development paradigm* (1st ed.). Emerald Group Publishing Limited.

Ziai, A. (2013). The discourse of "development" and why the concept should be abandoned. *Development in Practice, 23*(1), 123–136. https://doi.org/10.1080/09614524.2013.752792

Ziai, A. (2017). Post-development 25 years after the development dictionary. *Third World Quarterly, 38*(12), 2547–2558. https://doi.org/10.1080/01436597.2017.1383853

100 concrete steps to implement the 5 institutional reforms. (2015). http://www.kazakhembus.com/content/100-concrete-steps-implement-5-institutional-reforms#sthash.f78O3afG.dpuf

Index

N. Insebayeva, *Modernity, Development and Decolonization of Knowledge in Central Asia*, Politics and History in Central Asia,
https://doi.org/10.1007/978-981-16-5117-5

The manufacturer's authorised representative in the EU is Springer Nature Customer Service Centre GmbH, Europaplatz 3, 69115 Heidelberg, Germany. If you have any concerns regarding our products, please contact ProductSafety@springernature.com

Printed and bound by CPI Group (UK) Ltd, Croydon, CR0 4YY
30/09/2026
02225260-0007